# *in* Japanese

## The all-in-one language and travel guide

### Akiko Motoyoshi

#### Michael Houser

BBC Books

Developed by BBC Languages
Series adviser: Derek Utley
Audio producer: John Green, tefl tapes
Concept design by Carroll Associates
Typeset and designed by Manor Farm Design

Cover design by Carroll Associates
Cover photo: Pictor International – London

ISBN 0 563 40050 1

Published by BBC Books, a division of BBC Worldwide Ltd
First published 1998

Printed and bound in Great Britain by Cambus Litho, East Kilbride
Colour separations by DOT Gradations, Chelmsford

**Photographs**
All photographs by Akiko Motoyoshi, except the following:

Getty Images: 12, 13(b)
Michael Houser: p2, 5(t), 8(l), 14(t), 21(l), 30(t), 31(t), 36, 39(m),
45(b), 79(t), 80(bl), 83(t), 88(b)?, 95(m), 102(b)
The Image Bank: spine, back (t)
Pictor International – London: back (m), p13(t)
Rex Features: back (b)

Kana by Kaneyoshi: p1, 16, 24, 34, 44, 56, 64, 76, 79, 90, 102

Akiko Motoyoshi wishes to thank Karen Parr for her help with
the book.
Due to the scale of the map, it has not been possible to include full
details; however, every care has been taken to include as many of the
places mentioned in the book as possible.

## INTRODUCTION

*Get By in Japanese* will enable you to pick up the language, travel with confidence and experience the very best the country has to offer. You can use it both *before* a trip, to pick up the basics of the language and to plan your itinerary, and *during* your trip, as a phrasebook and as a source of practical information in all the key travel situations.

### Contents
**Insider's guide to Japan** An introduction to the country, a guide to the main cities and highlights for planning itineraries.
**Bare necessities** The absolute essentials of Japanese.
Seven main chapters covering key travel situations from *Getting around* to *Entertainment and leisure*. Each chapter has three main sections: *information* to help you understand the local way of doing things; *Phrasemaker*, a phrasebook of key words and phrases; *Language works / Try it out*, simple dialogues and activities to help you remember the language.
**Menu reader** A key to menus in Japanese.
**Doing business** A straightforward guide to business protocol.
**Language builder** A simple introduction to Japanese grammar.
**1000-word dictionary** The most important Japanese words you will come across with their English translations.
**Japanese syllabet** The hiragana and katakana equivalents of rōmaji syllables.
**Sounds Japanese** A clear guide to pronouncing the language.

### How to use the book
**Before you go** You can use the *Insider's guide* to get a flavour of the country and plan where you want to go. To pick up the language, the *Phrasemaker* sections give you the key words and phrases; the Language works dialogues show the language in action, and Try it out offers you a chance to practise for yourself.
**During your trip** *The Insider's guide* offers tips on the best things to see and do in the main cities. The *Phrasemaker* works as a phrasebook with all the key language to help you get what you want. Within each chapter there is also practical 'survival' information to help you get around and understand the country.

# Insider's guide to Japan

## Historical context

Japan's history provides valuable insights into the mind-set of contemporary Japan. Spoken Japanese preceded a means of writing it by much longer than in other countries (Japan's earliest historical records date only from the eighth century) with the result that myth permeates much of Japanese historical consciousness. The ruling Yamato dynasty, for instance, is believed to have provided all of Japan's purported 125 *mikado* (emperors), dating back to the seventh century BC and the sun goddess Amaterasu; in reality, the notions of an emperor and nationhood in Japan only date from the sixth century AD, and there is archaeological evidence of early civilisation in Japan going back to 11,000 BC.

Japanese still use the *gengō*, or regnal dating system, for official purposes, defining a given year in terms of the current Emperor's reign. The Heisei Era, the present official period, began in 1989. Accordingly, 1999 in Japan is the year Heisei 11 and 2001 will be Heisei 13.

Chinese influence, beginning in the seventh century AD, brought Buddhism, an ideographic writing system and the seeds of high culture to Japan. The imperial capital, based in Heian (Kyōto) from the ninth century, became the centre of a rich aesthetic culture which provided the foundation for Japanese excellence in the expressive arts. Many of these – *Noh* theatre, landscape architecture, *ikebana* (flower arranging), *cha-no-yu* (tea ceremony), brush writing and ink painting – flourished in the three centuries leading up to the first contact between Japan and the West.

This is reputed to have been in 1543, when Portuguese seamen (described at the time as *Nanbanjin* or 'barbarians from the south') were washed up onto islands south of Kyūshū. However, by the 1630s, Japan's de facto ruler, the *shōgun* (military supremo) had expelled all but a handful of Dutch and Chinese merchants. So successfully was Japan sealed off from contact with the 'outside' world that the seal remained unbroken until 1853, when the American Commodore Matthew Perry presented Japan with an offer it was technologically powerless to refuse. Foreigners were known then – and still are known – as *gaijin*, literally 'people from outside'.

From 1868, Japan embarked on a crash-course in re-inventing itself, using Europe and North America as its models. Within the span of only two generations, the then-current image of a quaint and exotic Japan was transformed in the world's consciousness into that of a major industrial and colonial power.

In the aftermath of the Second World War, Japan rose phoenix-like to become the first economy in Asia to industrialize fully. By the 1970s, it was a by-word for high-tech manufacturing, and in the 1980s, it became the oracle of new management ideas such as Continuous Improvement, Just-In-Time and Consensus Management.

Following the collapse of its 'Bubble Economy' in 1990, throughout the first half of the 1990s Japan suffered its worst recession since the Great Depression; yet it remains the world's second largest economy.

# Geographic context

Japan has often been characterised as 'Asia's Britain' because its development, its language and aspects of its culture set it apart from its neighbours on the East Asian mainland. The 1,861-mile-long Japanese archipelago lies 125 miles off the coast of East Asia, in a single time zone which places Japan nine hours ahead of GMT and 14 hours ahead of New York; there is no summer time, and Japan's clocks are never moved forward or backward.

Roughly the size of California or Sweden, Japan is pre-eminently an island nation, comprising four principal islands (from north to south: Hokkaidō, Honshū, Shikoku and Kyūshū) and thousands of smaller ones. The largest of these are the Ryūkyūs in the south, of which Okinawa is the best known. The Kuriles, north-east of Hokkaidō, are better known to the Japanese as the Northern Territories, and are the subject of a bitter and continuing dispute with Russia, which has occupied them since the dying days of the Second World War (there is still no peace treaty).

Japan's principal geographic dimensions are north-south. It sits in an unstable geological zone over the juncture of the Eurasia and Pacific Plates which, Japanese seismologists claim, induce a major quake in Japan every 69 years (although the last, prior to the Hanshin Quake in 1995, was the Great Kantō Quake of 1923). Upwards of 80 per cent of Japan's landmass is mountainous; the Japanese Alps run down the middle of the largest island, Honshū, acting as the 'spine of Japan'; the tallest mountain is Mount Fuji, an inactive volcano rising 12,390 feet, although there are some 50 active volcanoes, with Mount Aso and Mount Sakurajima (both in Kyūshū) being the best known.

The country enjoys pronounced seasonality, the Pacific coast being warmer in winter and wetter in summer than what the Japanese call the 'back of Japan', the Japan Sea coast. April, May and October are the most comfortable times of the year to visit.

paddy fields

# Cultural and ethnic context

Meiji Jingū shrine, Tōkyō

Because it is not nearly as racially or ethnically diverse as developed nations in Europe, North America or Australasia, the label 'homogeneous' is often pinned on Japan, leading to stereotypes which the Japanese themselves have, if anything, encouraged. Ninety-nine per cent or more of the population is ethnic Japanese, with low immigration and naturalisation rates; surprisingly, only about ten per cent of the population have passports.

The number of Europeans, North Americans and Australians found in Japan is far less than the number of Japanese found in New York, London, Melbourne or Los Angeles. Ethnically and culturally, however, there is more diversity than first meets the eye.

The largest non-Japanese ethnic population is Korean, numbering possibly a million, many of whom were born in Japan and speak Japanese as their first language; there are a further 100,000 ethnic Chinese. The first inhabitants of the Japanese archipelago, the aboriginal *Ainu*, number a few tens of thousands, living mainly in Hokkaidō. The descendants of Japan's medieval untouchable caste, the *Eta* (*burakumin* in Japanese PC-speak), are invisible to outsiders . . . but not to the Japanese.

The ethnic and racial mix of Japan is diversifying as a result of Japan's economic success and the need to attract – or turn a blind official eye to – immigrant 'guest workers' willing to do the menial, unskilled jobs today's well-educated Japanese no longer countenance.

roadside Buddha

# Money

The unit of currency in Japan is the Yen, identified by ¥; there are no limits on the amount of Yen or foreign currencies you may bring with you into Japan, but there is a ¥5m limit on how much you may take out. Unlike other parts of Asia, US dollars are not acceptable in cash transactions. Yen come in coin denominations of ¥1, ¥5, ¥10, ¥50, ¥100 and ¥500, and ¥1,000, ¥5,000 and ¥10,000 note denominations (10,000, or *man*, is a basic unit in

Japanese counting).

For security while en route and convenience while in Japan, it is advisable to obtain traveller's cheques before your departure. US Dollar-denominated traveller's cheques take longer to exchange than Yen-denominated ones, but unused Dollar cheques are more practical elsewhere.

Foreign exchange transactions can be made easily on arrival at Narita or Kansai International

field workers, Hokkaido

airports, at 'city' banks (banks such as Sakura or Tōkyō-Mitsubishi, which have national branch networks) and main post offices displaying *Authorised Foreign Exchange* signs (in English) and, if you're prepared to pay more for the privilege, at major hotels and department stores. Don't go to banks until after 10.30 am, when foreign departments open.

Japan is a cash-carrying society, and the low crime rates allow you to follow suit without worry. Personal cheques are unknown, but pre-paid smart cards are popular with the Japanese. Credit cards have come into increasing use in the past 20 years, with JCB Cards, Amex, Diner's Club and Visa (more so than MasterCard) all being widely accepted. Do not purchase on the assumption that a credit card will be accepted – always ask first, especially in smaller businesses.

If you use your credit card to obtain a cash advance from an ATM (cash machine), remember that, with few exceptions, ATMs in Japan shut down by 7 pm (banks believe they should only be in service while someone is still inside the bank to deal with breakdowns or faults). In major cities, however, it is sometimes possible to withdraw cash 24 hours a day with a Visa or Mastercard.

# Entry requirements and visas

Visitors from Britain and Eire do not require visas for (non-working) visits of less than 180 days (though on arrival, you are likely to be granted an initial, extendible stay of 90 days). For visitors from Canada, the United States and New Zealand, this period is limited to 90 days.

Visitors from Australia and South Africa must obtain a visa, which is issued free on presentation of passport-sized photos and a ticket for onward or return travel. Working Holiday Visas are available to Australians, Canadians and New Zealanders aged 18–25 for six months (extendible), provided employment is part-time or temporary.

For stays of any kind longer than 90 days, an Alien Registration Card (*gaikokujin tōroku shōmeisho*) is required, obtainable from the Municipality Ward Office where you reside. Don't be shocked when you are fingerprinted – this is standard procedure; the ARC must be carried with you at all times.

No inoculations are required, but if you are travelling to rural areas and during summer months, seek advice from your doctor before you travel about protection against hepatitis B and Japanese B encephalitis.

In general, if you think you'll be staying longer than 90 days, take a supply of passport-sized colour photos (1cm x 2cm).

# Tōkyō

Tōkyō Tower

*T*ōkyō will challenge your senses on first contact – the sprawl, the prevailing mood of greyness and concrete, the lack of a readily apparent centre, the absence of greenery and open space, the sheer scale of the place. Like most first-time visitors' reactions to Japan, you need to re-tune your senses, learn to focus on detail and look beneath the surface. You will then begin to experience Tōkyō's character and energy, and to understand the logic behind its layout.

Until the imperial capital was moved there in 1868 (Tōkyō means 'eastern capital') from Kyōto as part of the Meiji modernisation, the town was known as Edo (estuary). Between 1603, when the great shōgun *Tokugawa Ieyasu* opted to transform what was then a sleepy fishing town into his principal residence, and 1868, Edo grew into one of the world's largest cities, developing a character of its own. First-time visitors are sometimes disappointed at the apparent absence of 'old Japan' in Tōkyō, perhaps unaware that Tōkyō was devastated in the Great Kantō Quake of 1923 and again in 1944/45 through fire-bombing. Tōkyō is the face of modern Japan, with the soul of old Japan just below the surface.

There is so much to see in Tōkyō that it makes sense to organise trips to specific areas where visits to several places can be combined in one outing. For short stays, it's sensible to remain within the area contained within the 29-station Yamanote Line, the JR surface train service which loops central Tōkyō.

If you think of the Imperial Palace/Marunouchi/Ginza areas as Tōkyō's most central zone, areas to the east and to the immediate *north/east (Tsukiji, Jinbōchō, Akihabara, Ueno, Asakusa and Nippori) are* **shitamachi** *(working-class) areas where you can experience what remains of the ambience and streetlife of 'old Tōkyō'. To the west lie the fashionable, hi-tech commercial and entertainment* **yamanote** *(uptown) districts (Shinjuku, Harajuku, Shibuya, Aoyama, Akasaka, Roppongi, Ikebukuro) which feature so prominently in Western media reports on Japan.*

## Don't miss

### Central
■ **Imperial Palace** (Ōtemachi) Sunday is the best day because the area is closed to traffic (known as *Pedestrian's Heaven*); the five-kilometre jogging course around the inner moat is fun to do.
■ **Sony Museum** (Yūrakuchō) If you can't leave Japan without a dose of very hi-tech, this is the best place in town to get a glimpse of how Japan envisages the 21st century.

### East
■ **Tsukiji Fish Market** (Tsukiji) This requires an early-morning call (arrive by 8 am) and appropriate footwear (wellies if you can, but plastic sandals are a good alternative – at any rate, anything

washable) but affords an interesting glimpse of Japan at work; a de rigueur follow-up is a sushi breakfast (see p9), followed by a visit to the nearby **Hama Rikyū Gardens** (thought to be the best in Tōkyō). You can then 'cruise' (catch a water taxi from Rikyū Teien) up the Sumida Gawa to **Asakusa**, capital of *shitamachi* Tōkyō.

### North/East
■ **Sensō-Ji Temple** (Asakusa) Despite being a modern replica, it is the magnet which draws you into one of the most interesting places to sample the atmosphere of Old Tōkyō on foot; if you want to see Edo-style buildings, go to nearby Nippori – you're also not far from the **Shitamachi History Museum** *(Shitamachi Fūzoku Shiryōkan)* in Ueno, well worth a visit if you've enjoyed Asakusa.
■ **Ueno Kōen** (Ueno) If you've had enough of neon, noise and tarmac, this is the best place to catch up on a bit of tranquillity, open spaces and

Imperial Palace

greenery; in early/mid-April, it's also the best place to witness *hanami*, the annual celebration of the cherry blossom, though in considerably less tranquil conditions. The Tōkyō National Museum – Japan's largest – is located in the grounds; if you

'bamboo shoots'

have to limit yourself to a single museum while in Japan, this should be it.

■ **Jinbōchō** (Jinbōchō/Kanda) A wonderful place for walking and browsing in the many bookshops and printshops for which this area is justifiably famed.

■ **Akihabara** (Akihabara) 'Electric City', home to countless electrical and electronic goods wholesalers. This is Tōkyō at its most brash, from the gaudy neon signs which blaze everywhere to the incessant touting (hand-held loudspeakers) which spills right into the street.

## West/North

■ **Yoyogi Kōen** (Harajuku) On Sunday afternoons, 'bamboo shoots' (young Japanese who shed their school gear to become 'rockabillies', so called because of the speed with which this happens) strut their stuff in a striking display of East meets West.

■ **Shinjuku** A city-within-a-city, Shinjuku is home to a clutch of skyscrapers, such as the NS Building, the Sumitomo Building and, tallest of all, the Tōkyō Metropolitan Government Offices. They afford panoramic views of the Tōkyō skyline (if you choose a clear day, you have a chance of seeing Mount Fuji). Shinjuku also has another side if you want to experience Japan-sleaze, in which case head for kabuki-chō, Tōkyō's red-light district. If you need a cover story to explain why you went there, it's also home to some of the best restaurants in Tōkyō.

■ **Meiji Jingū** (Shibuya/Harajuku) Arguably the most compelling shrine in Japan, set in tranquil grounds not far from the site of the 1964 Tōkyō Olympic Games.

■ **Ikebukuro** If you fancy a bit of shopping but time is limited, visit Tōbu or Seibu *depāto* in Ikebukuro – you could spend a whole day in either – and catch the Tōkyō skyline from the top of the Sunshine City Building.

## Cafés and restaurants

There are so many restaurants, cafés, bars and clubs in Tōkyō that you'll be really spoilt for choice. You can find any food imaginable, but you'll probably find Japanese dishes better value. And as you're in Asia, you should take the opportunity to try foods that are not available in the West; you'll also get a little closer to the 'real Japan' you're probably after. Don't be afraid to follow your instincts if you find a place which looks intriguing. For tips, *Tōkyō Journal* is an excellent source, especially for unusual foods, while *Tōkyō Time Out* (both monthly) provides background articles as well as information on restaurants and evening entertainment.

## Have breakfast in

■ **Sushi-sei** (Tsukiji 3541 7720) If you're visiting the fish market at Tsukiji, don't miss a trip to Sushi-sei (from 8 am) to have a breakfast like you've never had before.

## Have lunch in

■ **Genroku** (Harajuku 3498 3968) on the Omote Sandō is widely regarded as the premier *kaiten zushi* (sushi by the plate, chosen off a conveyor belt which winds its way past you as you sit at the counter) in Tōkyō, ideal for a quick lunch.
■ **Kanda Yabu Soba** (Kanda 3251 0287) Reputedly the best buckwheat noodles in town.

## Have dinner in

■ **Seryna** (Roppongi 3402 1051) Good if you like meat. *Shabu-shabu* and *teppan yaki* (in Mon Cher Ton Ton, in the basement) are a speciality; lovely Japanese interior decor, though you pay for it.
■ **Tsunahachi** (Shinjuku 3352 1012) is wallet-challenging but good value if you want the best *tenpura*.
■ **Tatsumiya** (Asakusa 3842 7373) Not far from the Sumida Gawa cruise boats, this restaurant offers *nabe* (stockpot) cuisine in Edo-period surroundings; good *shitamachi* value.
■ **Sasa no Yuki** (Negishi/JR Uguisudani 3873 1145) A vegetarian's nirvana, serving exclusively tofu-based dishes in every conceivable form, including starters (tofu soup), main courses (*tofu sutēki*), tofu salad and desserts (tofu pie).
■ **Nanbantei** (Roppongi 3402 0606) *Yakitori* cooked as you sit round open charcoal pits; worth visiting for its name alone, which means 'Inn of the Southern Barbarians'.
■ **Edogin** (Tsukiji 3543 4406) combines *sushi* right off the boat with big portions, keen prices and Old-Edo atmosphere.

Shinjuku

## Bars and clubs

The pace of life in Tōkyō accelerates once darkness falls; like the neon which blazes seemingly everywhere, the atmosphere is charged with human energy, the streets awash with swarms of young clubbers and older *sararīmen* (Japanese businessmen), hunting in packs. Roppongi, the heart of disco-Tōkyō, only comes alive when the sun goes down.

The sheer number of bars and clubs packed into backstreet warrens gives Tōkyō a distinctive character. Bars and discos, particularly in the *yamanote* (Akasaka, Ginza, Roppongi and Shinjuku) areas, can get very crowded and smoky; clubs cost more but can give more in return, especially jazz clubs, a particular Tōkyō favourite. For tips, look out for *Tour Companion* (weekly), *Tōkyō City Guide* (bi-weekly) and *Tōkyō Weekender* (weekly), geared to what's-on information and available free from major hotels and Tōkyō Tourist Information Centre. If you're on the prowl for *karaoke*, the best advice is to follow your ears.

■ **The Blue Note Tōkyō** (Aoyama) isn't the cheapest jazz club in town, but it attracts international talent.

■ **Kamiya** (Asakusa) is purportedly the oldest bar in Japan; it also serves food.

■ **Henry Africa** (Akasaka) is a pricey but peaceful, atmospheric *gaijin* bar.

■ **Le Club** (Minami-Azabu) super-stylish and very *shibui* (with an air of refined austerity), said to be the most elegant bar in Tōkyō.

■ **Akasaka Prince Sky Lounge** (Akasaka) has a piano bar on the top floor which offers a bird's-eye view of Tōkyō's lights.

## Day trips and excursions

**North**

■ **Nikkō/Mashiko** Nikkō is the mountain site of the 350-year-old mausoleum of Tokugawa Ieyasu, the great *shōgun* who united Japan by sealing it off from the world. The setting enhances the visual impact of the Tōshō-gū Shrine, its large stone *torii*, and the Shin Kyō bridge. If you have more than a day, you can consider hill walking, a visit to the Kegon Waterfall or *onsen* (see p36) at Lake Chūzenji-ko, both less than an hour away. Still further afield (east of Utsunomiya), Mashiko, made famous by world-renowned potter Shōji Hamada, is a must if you are into Japanese pottery.

■ **Tsukuba Science City** Dubbed the 'city of brains' by locals, this is the first of a series of futuristic technopolis (a second is taking shape north of Kōbe) built on virgin farmland in Ibaraki Prefecture. If you're interested in seeing how the Japanese plan a new town from scratch and in their approach to the post-industrial future, you'll find a brief visit here worthwhile.

## South

■ **Kamakura** For 150 years (1185–1333), Kamakura was Japan's national capital. It is famously associated with a major expansion of Buddhism throughout Japan. What draws innumerable visitors is the 750-year-old, 40 foot-high *Daibutsu* (Great Buddha). There are enough other shrines and temples to make an interesting day out.

## West

■ **Hakone/Fuji Five Lakes** Weather is all-important for this excursion since one of the main aims is to escape from urban Japan and admire that most traditional symbol of Japanese civilisation, Mount Fuji. A trip to the Hakone region is all about cruising Lake Ashino-ko (with Fuji-san providing the impressive backdrop), cablecar rides on Mount Komagatake and Mount Sōun-zan, where at Ōwakudani you can see volcanic hot springs. There is also the Chōkoku-no-mori open-air museum (pricey).

Closer to Fuji-san but still accessible in a (long) day, are the five lakes lying to the north of Fuji. Climbing Mount Fuji itself is a quintessential Japanese experience, though at 12,389 feet, not one that everyone is able or willing to have; you can ride to

within 4,265 feet of the top by cable car if you want. Even during the official climbing season (July–August, when the number of 'climbers' averages 5,000 daily) it will be near-freezing at the top, so make sure you take the right gear. The view is best at sunrise, so allow an excursion of several days. For your Japanese fellow-climbers, the journey is largely an emotional cultural pilgrimage which you can enjoy sharing.

Asakusa, see p7

# Kyōto

statue of Dōzō

*O*nce you know what to look for, Kyōto is closer to the mental picture of Japan that first-time visitors have until they hit Tōkyō. Happily, the city's unique 1,200-year-old cultural heritage was preserved thanks to the fact that Kyōto was not heavily bombed during the Second World War. This heritage comprises several thousand temples and shrines, the most famous landscape gardens in Japan, wooden houses evocative of Old Japan, excellent food and an entertainment culture popularly associated with kimonos, geisha and Noh drama.

Kyōto is laid out in a grid, perhaps the first sign of Chinese influence you encounter. There are so many temples and shrines that the best way to see the city is to walk, confining yourself to outings targeted on the central, northern and eastern parts of the city.

## Don't miss

**Centre**

■ **Pontochō** The central entertainment quarter containing tea houses, exclusive restaurants and *geisha* houses (some off-limits to foreigners).

■ **Imperial Palace** This is where Japan's emperors are enthroned. You need to make advance arrangements to visit.

■ **Nijō Palace** The Kyōto residence of the Tokugawa *shōgun*, designed to symbolize the *shōgun's* superior power and keep suspect feudal lords under surveillance.

**East**

■ **Kiyomizu Dera** Dating from the *sakoku* (seclusion) period, this is particularly striking for its enormous hillside wooden veranda which affords good views over the rooftops of Kyōto. The approach to it through 'Teapot Lane' is fun.

■ **Sanjūsangen-dō Temple** Vaguely reminiscent of a northern European long-house, it is distinctive for the 1,001 Buddhist statues it houses.

■ **Gion** The corner of Kyōto where you may see kimono-clad *maiko* (apprentice *geisha*) on their way to work; also where traditional entertainments (*Nihon buyō* – dance, *koto* and *gagaku* music, *kyōgen* – comic plays and *bunraku* – puppetry) are performed for tourists (at tourist prices).

■ **Ginkaku-ji Temple** The Silver Pavilion, like the Golden Pavilion (see p13), constructed in the late 15th century as a shogunal retreat, later converted into a temple.

**North/West**

■ **Ryōan-ji Temple** Its main attraction is the stone (*sansui* or 'dry landscape' style) garden; see if you can 'hear the sound of one hand clapping' after spending some time deep in meditation there.

■ **Heian Jingū** Brash (by Kyōto standards – vermilion was a popular court colour long ago) re-creation of the Imperial Palace from the Heian Period (794–1185).

■ **Daitoku-ji Temple** Houses a complex of some two dozen smaller temples and affords you a close encounter with Zen culture and the enterprise culture which (regrettably) surrounds Japanese religions of all hues.

■ **Kinkaku-ji Temple** The Golden Pavilion (recognisable because it actually looks golden). Like the Ginkaku-ji, it was originally (1397) constructed as a retreat, later converted into a temple and burnt down in 1950 by a deranged monk. *You* may need to retreat from the massive crowds it attracts.

## Restaurants

Kyōto is the home of *Kyō ryōri* (a variation on *kaiseki* with its emphasis on variety, presentation and superlative service) and *shōjin ryōri* (Japanese vegetarian cuisine, virtually vegan), so eating Japanese is a must.

Accordingly, you can choose from temple restaurants, small backstreet family restaurants in the Pontochō and

Gion quarters or splash out at some of the most expensive *kaiseki* restaurants in Japan.

## Have a meal in

■ **Junsei** (Nanzen-ji Temple 075 761 2311) Among the oldest of numerous restaurants offering Buddhist cuisine within the temple precinct; another favourite among vegetarians a few minutes' walk north is **Okutan** (075 771 8709), in the Chōshō-in Temple.

■ **Minokichi** (Pontochō 075 771 4185) Renowned for its *kaiseki*, it also offers you a chance to glimpse if not mingle with the key players in Japanese business and politics, among whom it is justifiably very popular.

■ **Yamatomi** (Pontochō 075 221 3268) Dine on a veranda overlooking the Kamo Gawa at sensible prices; *teppin-age*, which you cook for yourself at the table, is the house speciality.

■ **Gontarō** (Pontochō 075 221 5810) If you like pasta, try this restaurant which specialises in hand-made noodles.

Kiyomizu Temple

# Holidays, festivals and events

Gion Matsuri, Kyōto

The Japanese are proud of their image as workaholics. The reality, however, is that Japan has more public holidays (15) than any other developed nation; there is at least one public holiday in every month except June and August.

Four public holidays are incorporated into three periods of the year when most Japanese are not at work . . . and very possibly travelling (advance travel and accommodation reservations are essential at these times). From 29 April–5 May, Japan celebrates a 'Golden Week' encompassing four holidays. From 13–15 August, o-bon (Festival of the Dead) provides a break from the heat and humidity of mid-summer; although it is not a public holiday, practically all Japanese take some of their annual leave at this time. 28 December–5 January is the New Year break. Christmas is a working day rather than a holiday in Japan, though you might not believe it given the street decorations and festive lighting in all major cities.

## Main events

April marks the beginning of a new cycle of social life throughout Japan. Schools and universities reconvene, businesses begin their new financial years. Throughout April, Japan's TV weather forecasters nightly trace the northerly progress of the 'Cherry Blossom Front', which Japanese everywhere celebrate with *hanami*, boozy outdoor rites-of-spring parties. In Tōkyō, the place to be is Ueno Park.

Festivals abound throughout the year, providing a modern link with Japan's pre-industrial rural ways and with the country's only indigenous religion, *Shintō*. Before industrialization, *matsuri* (festivals) generally took place in the spring and autumn, to implore or thank the gods of nature for a bountiful harvest. In post-industrial Japan, festivals fill the calendar. The best incorporate elements of carnival, pageant parades and period re-enactments.

Among the many interesting and spectacular festivals in the Japanese calendar are the *Takoage* (kite-flying festival) at Hamamatsu and the *Tōshō-gū* Shrine Grand Festival at Nikko (17–18 May) which features latter-day *samurai* in full armour, celebrating the coming of the remains of the *Shōgun* Tokugawa Ieyasu in the 17th century. Tōkyō's *Sanja Matsuri*, staged around Asakusa's Kannon Temple (Sensō-ji) throughout the third weekend in May, is the most colourful pageant of working-class Tōkyō; the *Kanda Matsuri*, held the previous weekend, is Tōkyō's biggest.

Summer festivals were originally designed to ward off plague. The most famous and lengthy festival in all Japan is the 1,100-year-old *Gion Matsuri*, celebrated in Kyōto

kodo drummers

throughout July, and culminating in several spectacular days (and nights!) in mid-July. On the last Saturday in July, the *Sumida Gawa Hanabi Taikai* in Asakusa, Tōkyō, is a spectacular river fireworks celebration. The *Tenjin Matsuri* (24–25 July), at Ōsaka's Tenman Shrine, is one of the big three festivals in the Japanese calendar.

The most spectacular winter festival is the five-day-long *Yuki Matsuri* (Snow Festival) held in early (5–11) February in Sapporo, capital of the northernmost island, Hokkaidō, and scene of the 1972 Winter Olympic Games. The high point is the snow-sculpture competition using snow removed from the city's streets. On 15 November, *Shichi-Go-San* (festival of three-, five- and seven-year-olds) provides an opportunity everywhere in Japan to see children adorned in traditional dress. *Ganjitsu* (New Year's Day) is a private, family-oriented event in Japan, but on 2 January, the Imperial Palace in Tōkyō opens its grounds and gardens until mid-afternoon to catch a glimpse of the Imperial Family.

The following is a list of traditional Japanese festivals:

| Month | Festival | Where? |
|---|---|---|
| January | Hatsumōde | throughout the country |
| February | Ume matsuri | Yushima Shrine, Tōkyō |
| February | Yuki matsuri | Sapporo, Hokkaidō |
| April | Takayama Spring Festival | Takayama, Gifu |
| April/May | Onbashira matsuri | Nagano (every 6 years) |
| May | Aoi matsuri | Shimogamo Shrine, Kyōto |
| May | Sanja matsuri | Asakusa Shrine, Tōkyō |
| June | Mibu no hanadaue | Hiroshima |
| July | Gion matsuri | Yasaka Shrine, Kyōto |
| August | Tanabata | Sendai City, Miyagi |
| August | Nebuta | Aomori City, Aomori |
| September | Ōhara Hadaka matsuri | Ōhara Town, Chiba |
| October | Nagasaki Kunchi | Nagasaki City, Nagasaki |
| November | Hakone Daimyō Gyōretsu | Hakone Town, Kanagawa |
| December | Chichibu Night Festival | Chichibu City, Saitama |
| December | Hagoita ichi | Asakusa, Tōkyō |

Tanabata

Christmas shop window

# Bare necessities

## Greetings

| | |
|---|---|
| Good morning.<br>(until roughly 11 am) | **Ohayō gozaimasu.** |
| Hello/Good day/<br>Good afternoon.<br>(from 11 am until dusk) | **Konnichiwa.** |
| Good evening.<br>(after nightfall) | **Konbanwa.** |
| Good night.<br>(when turning<br>in for the night) | **Oyasumi nasai.** |
| Hello, I'm back.<br>(when you are arriving) | **Tadaima.** |
| Hello, welcome back.<br>(when someone else<br>is arriving) | **Okaeri nasai.** |
| Goodbye/Farewell. | **Sayōnara.** |
| Would you excuse me. | **Shitsurei shimasu.** |

## Other useful words

| | |
|---|---|
| yes | **hai** |
| yes (informal) | **un** |
| no | **iie** |
| No, thank you. | **Iie, kekkō desu.** |
| good/OK | **yoi/ii** |
| please | **dōzo/onegai shimasu** |
| thank you (informal) | **dōmo** |
| thank you (formal) | **arigatō/sumimasen** |
| Thanks a lot. | **Dōmo (arigatō/sumimasen).** |
| Thank you very much. | **Dōmo arigatō gozaimasu.** |
| Thank you very much<br>(for what you've done). | **Dōmo arigatō gozaimashita.** |
| You're welcome. | **Dō itashimashite.** |
| I'm sorry (for a minor thing). | **Sumimasen/Gomen nasai.** |
| I'm sorry (for something<br>more serious). | **Mōshiwake arimasen.** |
| Excuse me (to do something). | **Shitsurei shimasu.** |
| Pardon me (for something<br>you've done). | **Shitsurei shimashita/<br>Gomen nasai.** |

## At the dinner table

| | |
|---|---|
| when you start a meal (= thank you for this food) | **Itadakimasu** |
| when you have finished a meal (= thank you, that was delicious) | **Gochisōsama deshita** |

## Which, what, where and how

| | |
|---|---|
| How? | **Dono yōni/Dō yatte?** |
| How (many/much)? | **(Ikutsu/Dono gurai)?** |
| How often? | **Dono gurai yoku?** |
| How much is it? | **Ikura desu ka?** |
| How much (is this)? | **(Kore wa) ikura desu ka?** |
| What? | **Nani/Nan?** |
| Where? | **Doko?** |
| Where is it? | **Doko ni arimasu ka?** |
| Which . . . ? | **Dore/Dono . . . ?** |
| Where is (a public telephone)? | **(Kōshū denwa) wa doko ni arimasu ka?** |
| Where is the (toilet)? | **(Toire) wa doko desu ka?** |
| Where can I find (kimonos)? | **(Kimono) wa doko ni arimasu ka?** |
| Do you have any . . . ? | **. . . wa arimasu ka?** |

phone cards

## Getting things straight

| | |
|---|---|
| I don't understand. | **Wakarimasen.** |
| I beg your pardon? | **Mō ichido itte kudasai.** |
| Please speak slowly. | **Yukkuri itte kudasai.** |
| Do you speak English? | **Eigo wa dekimasu ka?** |
| I don't speak Japanese. | **Nihongo wa dekimasen.** |
| May I take photographs? | **Shashin o tottemo iidesu ka?** |
| May I smoke? | **Tabako o suttemo iidesu ka?** |

## About yourself

| | |
|---|---|
| How do you do? | **Hajimemashite.** |
| Pleased to meet you. | **Yoroshiku.** |
| (the more senior you are, the | **Dōzo yoroshiku.** |
| shorter the phrase you use) | **Dōzo yoroshiku onegai shimasu.** |
| | **Dōzo yoroshiku onegai itashimasu.** |
| I'm (Smith). | **(Sumisu) desu.** |
| I'm from (the UK). | **(Igirisu) kara kimashita.** |
| I'm a (businessman). | **(Bijinesuman) desu.** |
| My wife is a (lawyer). | **Tsuma wa (bengoshi) desu.** |
| I'm single. | **Dokushin desu.** |
| I'm married. | **Kekkon shite imasu.** |
| I'm divorced.* | **Rikon shimashita.** |
| I have a child/children. | **Kodomo ga imasu.** |
| How old are you? | **Nansai desu ka?** |
| I'm (45) years old. | **(Yonjūgo) sai desu.** |

* Divorce is not considered a suitable topic of conversation in Japan. Use this phrase only when it is important to convey your exact marital status.

## About other people

| | |
|---|---|
| How are you? | **O-genki desu ka?** |
| I'm fine (thanks). | **Genki desu (okagesama de).** |
| Have you been busy? | **O-isogashii desu ka?** |
| Yes, I keep myself busy. | **Hai, okagesama de** |
| (= business is good) | **Isogashii desu.** |
| Congratulations. | **O-medetō gozaimasu.** |

## Countries and nationalities

| | |
|---|---|
| America | **Amerika: Amerikajin** |
| Australia | **Ōsutoraria: Ōsutorariajin** |
| Austria | **Ōsutoria: Ōsutoriajin** |
| Belgium | **Berugii: Berugiijin** |
| Britain | **Igirisu: Igirisujin** |
| Canada | **Kanada: Kanadajin** |
| China | **Chūgoku: Chūgokujin** |
| Democratic P. R. of Korea | **Chōsen: Chōsenjin** |
| Denmark | **Denmāku: Denmākujin** |
| England | **Ingurando: Ingurandojin** |
| Finland | **Finrando: Finrandojin** |
| France | **Furansu: Furansujin** |
| Germany | **Doitsu: Doitsujin** |
| Greece | **Girisha: Girishajin** |
| India | **Indo: Indojin** |
| Ireland | **Airurando: Airurandojin** |
| Italy | **Itaria: Itariajin** |
| Japan | **Nippon: Nihonjin** |
| Luxembourg | **Rukusenburugu: Rukusenburugujin** |
| Netherlands | **Oranda: Orandajin** |
| New Zealand | **Nyūjiirando: Nyūjiirandojin** |
| Norway | **Noruuē: Noruuējin** |
| Portugal | **Porutogaru: Porutogarujin** |
| Republic of Korea | **Kankoku: Kankokujin** |
| Russia | **Roshia: Roshiajin** |
| Scotland | **Sukottorando: Sukottorandojin** |
| South Africa | **Minami Afurika: Minami Afurikajin** |
| Spain | **Supein: Supeinjin** |
| Sweden | **Suuēden: Suuēdenjin** |
| Switzerland | **Suisu: Suisujin** |
| Wales | **Uēruzu: Uēruzujin** |

## Occupations

| | |
|---|---|
| bank clerk | **ginkōin** |
| businessman | **bijinesuman** |
| salaried businessman | **sarariiman** |
| civil servant | **kōmuin** |
| company employee | **kaishain** |
| doctor | **isha** |
| housewife | **shufu** |
| lawyer | **bengoshi** |
| sales person | **sērusuman** |
| student | **gakusei** |
| teacher | **kyōshi** |
| non-working/unemployed | **mushoku** |
| retired | **taishokusha** |

Sakura Bank

Asahi Bank

## Changing money

| | |
|---|---|
| Would you please exchange this money for me? | **Kore o ryōgae shite kudasai.** |
| Would you please exchange these (pounds Sterling) for Japanese Yen? | **Kono (pondo) o en ni ryōgae shite kudasai.** |

## Telling the time

| | | | | |
|---|---|---|---|---|
| 1 o'clock | **ichiji** | | 7 o'clock | **shichiji** |
| 2 o'clock | **niji** | | 8 o'clock | **hachiji** |
| 3 o'clock | **sanji** | | 9 o'clock | **kuji** |
| 4 o'clock | **yoji** | | 10 o'clock | **jūji** |
| 5 o'clock | **goji** | | 11 o'clock | **jūichiji** |
| 6 o'clock | **rokuji** | | 12 o'clock | **jūniji** |

| | | | | |
|---|---|---|---|---|
| 1 minute | **ippun** | | 40 minutes | **yonjuppun** |
| 2 minutes | **nifun** | | 45 minutes | **yonjūgofun** |
| 3 minutes | **sanpun** | | a quarter to | **jūgofun mae** |
| 10 minutes | **juppun/jippun** | | 50 minutes | **gojuppun** |
| 15 minutes | **jūgofun** | | ten minutes to | **juppun mae** |
| 20 minutes | **nijuppun** | | 55 minutes | **gojūgofun** |
| 30 minutes | **sanjuppun** | | five minutes to | **gofun mae** |

| | |
|---|---|
| twenty past (one) | **(ichiji) nijuppun sugi** |
| twenty to (one) | **(ichiji) nijuppun mae** |

| | |
|---|---|
| in the morning | **gozen** |
| in the afternoon | **gogo** |
| throughout the morning | **gozenchū** |
| evening | **yūgata** |
| night | **yoru** |
| yesterday | **kinō** |
| today | **kyō** |
| tomorrow | **ashita/asu** |
| What time? | **Nanji . . . ?** |
| What time is it? | **Nanji desu ka?** |
| When? | **Itsu . . . ?** |

# Numbers

| | | | |
|---|---|---|---|
| 1 | **ichi** | 18 | **jūhachi** |
| 2 | **ni** | 19 | **jūkyū/jūku** |
| 3 | **san** | 20 | **nijū** |
| 4 | **yon/shi** | 21 | **nijūichi** |
| 5 | **go** | 22 | **nijūni** |
| 6 | **roku** | 30 | **sanjū** |
| 7 | **nana/shichi** | 40 | **yonjū/shijū** |
| 8 | **hachi** | 50 | **gojū** |
| 9 | **kyū/ku** | 60 | **rokujū** |
| 10 | **jū** | 70 | **nanajū/shichijū** |
| 11 | **jūichi** | 80 | **hachijū** |
| 12 | **jūni** | 90 | **kyūjū** |
| 13 | **jūsan** | 100 | **hyaku** |
| 14 | **jūyon/jūshi** | 1,000 | **sen** |
| 15 | **jūgo** | 10,000 | **ichiman** |
| 16 | **jūroku** | 100,000 | **jūman** |
| 17 | **jūnana/jūshichi** | 1,000,000 | **hyakuman** |

(see Counters, pp108–109)

# Days of the week

| | |
|---|---|
| Sunday | **Nichiyōbi** |
| Monday | **Getsuyōbi** |
| Tuesday | **Kayōbi** |
| Wednesday | **Suiyōbi** |
| Thursday | **Mokuyōbi** |
| Friday | **Kinyōbi** |
| Saturday | **Doyōbi** |

# Months

| | |
|---|---|
| January | **Ichigatsu** |
| February | **Nigatsu** |
| March | **Sangatsu** |
| April | **Shigatsu** |
| May | **Gogatsu** |
| June | **Rokugatsu** |
| July | **Shichigatsu** |
| August | **Hachigatsu** |
| September | **Kugatsu** |
| October | **Jūgatsu** |
| November | **Jūichigatsu** |
| December | **Jūnigatsu** |

calendar, Meiji Shrine

## Days of the month

The first ten days of the month, along with the 14th, 20th and 24th, all have irregular names in Japanese. The rest are formed by combining the number with **-nichi** (day).

| | | | |
|---|---|---|---|
| 1st | **Tsuitachi** | 9th | **Kokonoka** |
| 2nd | **Futsuka** | 10th | **Tōka** |
| 3rd | **Mikka** | 15th | **Jūgonichi** |
| 4th | **Yokka** | 20th | **Hatsuka** |
| 5th | **Itsuka** | 24th | **Nijūyokka** |
| 6th | **Muika** | 25th | **Nijūgonichi** |
| 7th | **Nanoka** | 30th | **Sanjūnichi** |
| 8th | **Yōka** | | |

## Colours

| | |
|---|---|
| black | **kuro** |
| blue | **ao/burū** |
| brown | **chairo/buraun** |
| gold | **kin'iro/gōrudo** |
| green | **midori/guriin** |
| grey | **haiiro/gurē** |
| pink | **momoiro/pinku** |
| purple | **murasaki** |
| red | **aka** |
| silver | **gin'iro/shirubā** |
| white | **shiro** |
| yellow | **kiiro** |

food and drink for sale

## Line up

Draw a line to the corresponding Japanese phrase.

1 Thanks a lot.
2 I'm sorry.
3 I don't understand.
4 Please speak slowly.
5 Where is the toilet?
6 Congratulations!

a **Toire wa doko desu ka?**
b **Yukkuri itte kudasai.**
c **O-medetō gozaimasu.**
d **Wakarimasen.**
e **Dōmo arigato.**
f **Mōshiwake arimasen.**

## A date for your diary

What are the following dates in Japanese?
a 15 January
b 3 May
c 20 July
d 10 October
e 23 December

## Language works

**1** Greetings and introducing yourself
□ **Ohayō gozaimasu.**
■ **Ohayō gozaimasu.**
□ **Hajimemashite. Sumisu desu. Dōzo yoroshiku onegai shimasu.**
■ **Hajimemashite. Kurosawa desu. Dōzo yoroshiku.**

Is this the first meeting between you and Mr Kurosawa?
When does the meeting take place: in the morning or the afternoon?

**2** When you happen to see an acquaintance
□ **Konnichiwa.**
■ **Konnichiwa. O-genki desu ka?**
□ **Hai, genki desu okagesama de. O-isogashii desu ka?**
■ **Hai, okagesama de.**

Has your acquaintance been busy?

## Sound check

There are numerous dialects (eg **Ōsaka-ben**, **ben** = dialect) as well as regional accents in spoken Japanese. Japanese schools teach **kokugo**, a standard version of Japanese which is spoken throughout the Japanese archipelago, in addition to any dialects spoken in particular regions. **Kokugo** is always used when speaking to foreigners, so pronunciation is less likely to be a problem than speed.

# Getting around

| 羽田空港<br>Haneda Airport | 赤坂地区<br>Akasaka Area | 新宿地区<br>Shinjuku Area | 箱崎 TCAT<br>Tokyo City Air Terminal |
| 横浜 YCAT<br>Yokohama City Air Terminal | 品川・羽田東地区<br>Shinagawa/Ebisu Area | 池袋地区<br>Ikebukuro Area | 東京駅<br>Tokyo Station |

As a society, Japan simply could not function without highly organised and reliable transport systems; three million people pass through Shinjuku Station daily, and the world's busiest air routes are Tōkyō-Ōsaka and Tōkyō-Sapporo.

Buses, trains, ferries and planes are all at your disposal . . . not to mention rental cars, taxis, monorails, water taxis and, of course, your own two feet (in *The Roads to Sata*, Englishman Alan Booth tells what it's like to walk the length of the archipelago).

Making the most of the transport options Japan can offer depends on where you are, where you're going, how much time you have and how much you're prepared to pay.

## Airport-city transfers

If you arrive by air from abroad, you'll land at New Tōkyō International Airport, at Narita, 41 miles north-east of Tōkyō, or Kansai International Airport, Japan's new 24-hour hi-tech terminal in the Bay of Ōsaka. The latter affords quick and easy access to Ōsaka, Kōbe and Kyōto by 'limousine' bus (limo-bus), train or taxi.

Arriving at Narita is more complicated. If you're connecting to an internal flight, you will almost certainly need to transfer to Haneda Airport, two hours away by limo-bus; from Hamamatsu-chō station in central Tōkyō, there is a monorail service (journey time approximately 20 minutes) direct to Haneda.

You have various options (three rail services, limo-bus and taxi) for travel into Tōkyō. Taxis are far too expensive. The limo-bus offers the most frequent services to a variety of downtown locations, including major hotels and TCAT/YCAT (Tōkyō/Yokohama City Air Terminal), but depending on your arrival time, it can take up to two hours. Trains are the best option; frequency and speed (50 to 90 minutes' journey time) depend on how much you're willing to pay. Tuck away ¥2,040 to pay the airport departure tax before you fly home.

> Where is the JR station?
> **JR no eki wa doko desu ka?**

## Travel in the cities

In theory, you can drive, take buses, walk and, in Tōkyō, take the *suijō takushii* or water taxi.

The surface and underground rail systems are so comprehensive, reliable and cost effective that they are easily the preferred choice.

Terminal Connection Bus
ターミナル連絡バス

Japan's nine largest cities all have underground systems. These form part of an integrated urban mass transport system known as *kokuden*, a metropolitan surface loop rail line (the famous *Yamanote Sen*, in Tōkyō) which interfaces with underground and regional rail systems. The services are fast, reliable and frequent; the only drawbacks are crowding at peak hours and comparatively early shut-down. Station names are written in Roman script, and rail and underground trains come in different colours, conveniently corresponding to the colours used on transport maps. English-language versions of these are widely available, though bilingual versions are helpful since you need *kanji* station names to work out underground fares; if you're not certain of the fare, buy the cheapest ticket and if necessary pay any extra due at the Fare Adjustment Office (*ryōkin seisanjo*) where you get off.

*Tōkyō Free kippu* ('free ticket') is the term for a one-day unlimited travel pass; although they can be used on surface and underground trains, they cannot be used interchangeably. JR's *Orenji kādo* (Orange Card) is a pre-paid smart card which can be used in ticket vending machines, saving time and the need to carry change.

**!** Where can I buy a ticket?
**Kippu wa doko de kaemasu ka?**

Buses are not an attractive alternative to rail in the cities. Traffic congestion renders them a slow and laborious way of getting around, and services close down very early. They're also more difficult to use since the stops are announced in Japanese; try them if you're adventurous, but be sure to

TAXI
タクシーのりば

have your destination in *kanji* to show the driver as you board.

## Inter-city travel

Rail travel again offers the best option overall because the rail network is comprehensive, stations are conveniently located (main stations house travel agencies) and you have four or five different levels of service to match your budget.

The JR (Japan Railways) network covers the entire country, running some 25,000 trains a day; JR also runs buses and ferries. The range of services includes:

■ **futsū** or local service: the slowest trains which stop at all stations with no reserved seats and usually no air-conditioning (tickets are sold from vending machines)

■ **kyūkō** or ordinary express service: seats can be booked up to 30 days in advance.

■ **tokkyū** or special express service: faster, with fewer stops.

■ **shinkansen** or super express service (known to foreigners as the 'bullet train'), the jewel in JR's crown. The Tōkaidō Line runs south along the Pacific coast to northern Kyūshū, the Tōhoku Line runs north-east to Morioka in the far reaches of Honshū, and the Jōetsu Line runs north through the Japan Alps to Niigata. Each line offers a variety of high-speed services (from selected stops to all stations), with between four and six departures each hour to/from Tōkyō's Central and Ueno stations.

🔴 Which platform does the train for Tōkyō leave from?
🔴 **Tōkyō yuki wa nanbansen kara desu ka?**

The faster you travel, the more expensive it gets. Visitors may purchase *Japan Rail Passes* (seven-, 14- and 21-day varieties) which provide huge savings if you intend to travel a lot by rail (or JR buses and ferries). They must be purchased abroad (JAL offices sell them) and run from the moment you validate them in Japan (don't do it at Narita; wait until you're ready to travel outside Tōkyō). For more limited rail travel, *shūyūken kippu* (excursion tickets) offer savings; travel agencies offer packages which include cheaper rail travel, and discount agencies (consult the foreign-language press) sell cheaper tickets.

If you have the time and are particularly cost conscious, night buses and ferries are a further option. Don't try to take too much luggage on a night bus. Ferries are very cost effective though slow; Western Honshū-Kyūshū and Shikoku have the largest number of services but if you want, you can sail from Tōkyō as far as Hokkaidō or even Okinawa.

## Road travel

Renting a car or travelling by bicycle is not recommended in Japan's cities. If you are in a group and want to travel independently to out-of-the-way places, car hire is feasible, although you should be aware that all road signs are in *kanji*, which makes navigation difficult.

holiday brochure

The best strategy is to get close to your destination by rail then rent from there; rental agencies are usually located near stations and pricing rewards return rentals. You can drive on an international licence for up to twelve months and should consider getting a copy of *Rules of the Road* as well as a bilingual road atlas (Metropolitan Expressway maps in English are available at Narita Airport). Remember that the Japanese drive on the left.

Most important of all, plan somewhere interesting to drive to. Petrol and inter-city motorway tolls are both very expensive, and speed limits can be only 31 mph on lesser roads, so it only makes sense to drive if you're part of a group and you're rewarded by attractive scenery and access to interesting places. Plan short excursions: the Japan Alps, Hokkaidō and the Sea of Japan coast of Honshū are places to consider.

## Travel for disabled visitors

Although Japan offers better provision for disabled visitors than other countries in Asia, Japanese society's consciousness of the public needs of the disabled is more limited than in the West.

Major road crossings in the largest cities have audio speakers which play tunes when it is safe to cross; rail platforms have raised surfaces near the edge; newer public buildings are equipped with ramps for ease of access. But these, regrettably, are much the exception; particular care needs to be taken when travelling, which, because of possible hazards, should never be undertaken unaccompanied. Although Japanese hospitality to foreigners is legendary (money has been lent to complete strangers when ATMs are closed), it is not as forthcoming with the disabled; many Japanese simply don't appear to know what's expected of them.

## Understanding Japanese addresses

Unless you know the particular building or house you are visiting, locating an address in Japan should be regarded more as an adventure than a matter-of-fact routine. The majority of streets are simply not named or marked; addresses are often shared and are not necessarily consecutive. The basic logic underlying Japanese addresses is also fundamentally different from the West:

■ general areas are identified within an address in preference to specific locations.

■ you are expected to have to narrow down your search as you proceed; you may be given landmarks to locate a place rather than a specific street and number.

■ invariably, you will not locate your destination without the help of others, often policemen sitting in neighbourhood *kōban* (police boxes with red lights on top).

Because of the complexity of the system, most Japanese are very good at giving directions.

Take me to this address, please.
**Kono jūsho made onegai shimasu.**

# Phrasemaker

税関 (旅具通関部門) →
**CUSTOMS**

## At the airport

| | |
|---|---|
| Where is (the Tourist Information Centre/my luggage)? | **(Kankō annaijo/Watashi no nimotsu) wa doko desu ka?** |
| I have nothing to declare. | **Shinkoku suru mono wa nanimo arimasen.** |

| | |
|---|---|
| airport | **kūkō** |
| bureau de change | **ryōgaejo** |
| cash | **genkin** |
| traveller's cheque | **toraberāzu chekku** |
| taxi | **takushii** |
| bus | **basu** |
| airport shuttle ('limo') bus | **rimujin basu** |
| plane | **hikōki** |
| airline company | **kōkūgaisha** |

## At passport control

| | |
|---|---|
| **Hōmon no mokuteki wa nan desu ka?** | What's the purpose of your visit? |
| **Nihon niwa (dono/dore) gurai taizai no yotei desu ka?** | How long are you going to stay in Japan? |

| | |
|---|---|
| I'm here on business. | **Shigoto desu.** |
| I'm a tourist. | **Kankō desu.** |
| I plan to stay for (a week). | **(Isshūkan) taizai no yotei desu.** |

| | |
|---|---|
| **gaikokujin** | aliens/foreigners |
| **Nihonjin** | Japanese person |
| **nyūkoku shinsa** | passport control |
| **nyūkoku kādo** | disembarkation card |
| **binmei** | flight number |
| **zeikan** | customs |
| **ken'eki** | quarantine |
| **shukkoku** | embarkation |
| **shukkoku kādo** | embarkation card |

シティエアターミナル
Exit for
City Air Terminal

出口 1　東京シティエアターミナル
Tōkyō City Air Terminal
箱崎交番　リバーサイド読売ビル
Hakozaki Police Box　Riverside Yomiuri Bldg.
日本橋箱崎町　日本橋中洲
Nihombashi-hakozakichō　Nihombashi-nakazu

| | |
|---|---|
| (Non-smoking/Smoking), please. | **(Kin'enseki/Kitsuenseki) onegai shimasu.** |
| Do you have an (aisle/window) seat? | **(Tsūrogawa/Madogawa) no seki wa arimasu ka?** |
| What is the boarding time? | **Tōjō kaishi wa nanji desu ka?** |
| How long will it be delayed? | **Dore gurai okuremasu ka?** |

pedestrian bridge

## Using public transport

二重橋前駅
Nijūbashimae Sta.

日比谷駅
Hibiya Sta.

| | |
|---|---|
| ticket | **kippu** |
| taxi (rank) | **takushii (noriba)** |
| bus | **basu** |
| bus stop | **basutei** |
| car hire | **rentakā** |
| station | **eki** |
| Yamanote Line | **Yamanote Sen** |
| Tōkyō JR Station | **JR Tōkyō Eki** |
| underground | **chikatetsu** |

## Asking directions

| | |
|---|---|
| map | **chizu** |
| Where is the (station)? | **(Eki) wa doko desu ka?** |
| I'm looking for (a taxi rank). | **(Takushii noriba) o sagashite imasu.** |
| Is this a (Keisei Line) station? | **(Keisei Sen) no eki desu ka?** |
| Is there a (JR station) near here? | **(JR no eki) wa kono chikaku ni arimasu ka?** |
| Could you show me how to get to . . . ? | **. . . eno ikikata o oshiete kudasai.** |
| Is it (far/close)? | **(Tōi/Chikai) desu ka?** |
| How long does it take? | **Dore gurai kakarimasu ka?** |

off limits

立入禁止

| | |
|---|---|
| **Koko desu.** | It's here. |
| **Soko desu.** | It's there. |
| **Asoko desu.** | It's over there. |
| **ue** | above |
| **(Migi/Hidari) desu.** | It's on the (right/left). |
| **Sono (shita/yoko) desu.** | It's (below/next to) it. |
| **massugu (yukimasu)** | (to go) straight on |
| **magarimasu** | to turn |
| **kita/minami** | north/south |
| **higashi/nishi** | east/west |
| **Wakarimasen.** | I don't understand. |
| **Chizu wa arimasu ka?** | Do you have a map? |
| **Jūsho wa nan desu ka?** | What's the address? |
| **Takushii ga ichiban ii desu.** | It's best to take a taxi. |
| **(Ichijikan) kakarimasu.** | It'll take (an hour). |
| **(Shingō) de migi e magatte kudasai.** | Turn right at the (traffic lights). |
| **. . . sorekara . . .** | . . . and then . . . |
| **(Futatsume no kado) de hidari e itte kudasai.** | Turn left at the (second turning). |
| **Ki o tsukete.** | Be careful! |

入口 entrance

## Places of interest

| | |
|---|---|
| amusement park | **yūenchi** |
| art gallery | **bijutsukan** |
| bank | **ginkō** |
| bridge | **hashi** |
| (Emperor's) palace | **kōkyo** |
| exhibition | **tenrankai** |
| hospital | **byōin** |
| hotel | **hoteru** |
| inn | **ryokan** |
| library | **toshokan** |
| museum | **hakubutsukan** |
| park | **kōen** |
| parliament | **kokkai gijidō** |
| petrol station | **gasorin sutando** |
| police box | **kōban** |
| post office | **yūbinkyoku** |
| restaurant | **resutoran** |
| river | **kawa** |
| school | **gakkō** |
| shrine | **jinja** |
| spa | **onsen** |
| swimming pool | **pūru** |
| temple | **(o-)tera** |
| Tōkyō Tower | **Tōkyō tawā** |
| university | **daigaku** |

Not a crossing

## Asking about bus and train services

| | |
|---|---|
| Where is the (bus stop/train) for . . . ? | **. . . yuki no (basutei/densha) wa doko desu ka?** |
| Where can I buy a ticket? | **Kippu wa doko de kaemasu ka?** |
| Is this a (bus/train) for . . . ? | **Kore wa . . . yuki no (basu/densha) desu ka?** |
| Is the next stop . . . ? | **Tsugi wa . . . desu ka?** |
| Where is the terminus? | **Shūten wa doko desu ka?** |
| What's the fare to . . . ? | **. . . made ryōkin wa ikura desu ka?** |
| When is the last service? | **Saishū wa nanji desu ka?** |

## Asking at the station

| | |
|---|---|
| Where is the ticket (counter/barrier)? | **(Kippu uriba/Kaisatsuguchi) wa doko desu ka?** |
| Which platform does the train for (Tokyo) leave from? | **(Tōkyō) yuki wa nanbansen kara desu ka?** |
| Is this a (non-smoking/first-class) carriage? | **Kore wa (kin'ensha/guriinsha) desu ka?** |
| Are these (reserved seats)? | **Kore wa (shiteiseki) desu ka?** |
| Which carriages have (non-reserved) seats? | **(Jiyūseki) wa dono sharyō desu ka?** |

| | |
|---|---|
| train | **densha** |
| bullet train | **shinkansen** |
| special/limited express | **tokkyū** |
| express | **kyūkō** |
| local service train | **futsū densha** |
| all-stations service | **kakueki teisha** |
| a (single/return) ticket | **(katamichi/ōfuku) kippu** |
| first class | **guriinsha** |
| non-smoking car | **kin'ensha** |
| non-smoking seat | **kin'enseki** |
| reserved seat | **shiteiseki** |
| timetable | **jikokuhyō** |

| | |
|---|---|
| **Nanmai desu ka?** | How many tickets? |
| **Katamichi desu ka, ōfuku desu ka?** | Single or return? |
| **(Jūni)bansen kara desu.** | It leaves from Platform (12). |
| **Tōkyō yuki desu.** | It's for Tokyo. |
| **Kippu o haiken shimasu.** | Tickets, please. |

## Getting to places by taxi

| | |
|---|---|
| (Narita Airport/Akasaka Hotel), please. | **(Narita Kūkō/Akasaka Hoteru) made onegai shimasu.** |
| Please stop here. | **Koko de tomete kudasai.** |
| Here is fine. | **Koko de kekkō desu.** |
| Would you wait for a moment? | **Chotto matte itte kudasai.** |
| Would you wait for (15 minutes)? | **(Jūgofun) matte itte kudasai.** |
| How much is the fare? | **Ryōkin wa ikura desu ka?** |
| Could I have a receipt, please? | **Ryōshūsho o onegai shimasu.** |

31

## Language works

**1** At passport control
■ **Hōmon no mokuteki wa nan desu ka?**
□ **Shigoto desu.**
■ **Nihon niwa dono gurai taizai no yotei desu ka?**
□ **Isshūkan desu.**

You are in Japan for a week on business: true/false?

**2** Finding your way to the station
□ **Sumimasen. Eki wa doko desu ka?**
■ **Massugu yukimasu. Kōen ga arimasu. Sono no yoko desu.**

Should you turn or go straight on? The station is next to the museum: true/false?

**3** Asking where the ticket office is
□ **Kippu uriba wa doko desu ka?**
■ **Asoko desu. Jikokuhyō ga arimasu. Sono shita desu.**

The ticket counter is underneath the timetable: true/false?

**4** Finding the right platform
□ **Tōkyō yuki wa nanbansen kara desu ka?**
■ **Jūnibansen kara desu.**

Which platform should you go to catch a train to Tōkyō?

**5** Finding out how long a journey takes
□ **Dono gurai kakarimasu ka?**
■ **Umm . . . ichijikan kakarimasu.**

How long does it take?

**6** Asking directions.
□ **Jūsho wa nan desu ka?**
■ **Aoyama 5-chōme 14 no 4 desu.**
□ **Takushii ga ichiban ii desu.**

Are you more likely to take a taxi or to walk to this address?

## Try it out

### Mix and match

Match up the corresponding Japanese terms.
1 map
2 ticket
3 Tourist Information Centre
4 bus
5 taxi rank
6 airport
7 station

a basu
b eki
c kūkō
d takushii noriba
e chizu
f kippu
g kankō annaijo

### Fill the gaps

Can you fill in the gaps in this conversation?
□ **Kono resutoran eno ikikata o** ..... (could you show me)?
■ **Jūsho wa nan desu ka?** . . . **Tōku arimasen.**
□ **Dore gurai kakarimasu ka?**
■ **Kokokara ni, san pun desu. Shingō de migi e magatte** . . . **Sorekara hidari e magatte kudasai.**
□ ..... (Traffic light) **de** ..... (right) **desu ne.**
■ **Hai.**
□ **Sorekara** ..... (left) **desu ne.**
■ **Hai, ki o tsukete.**
□ ..... (Thanks a lot.)

## Sound check

When reading romanised Japanese, remember:
■ that Japanese words are generally built on clusters of syllable sounds **(A/ka/sa/ka; Na/go/ya; Ni/ho/n)**
■ to read each syllable as a single sound, not as a combination of individual sounds.

To the East Kantō motorway

# Somewhere to stay

Japan has a number of world-class hotels: The Palace, The Imperial, the Akasaka Prince (great panoramic views), the Hotel Ōkura (Toranomon, Tōkyō), which even has its own museum, and the New Ōtani, which has a spectacular garden. Service is discrete and generally excellent; ancillary services on offer at top-class hotels are remarkable; although 'gifts' may be left for staff after a stay of several days at deluxe hotels, there is no tipping (a service charge is automatically added to your bill). Overall, the range of choice in terms of amenity, character and price is considerable.

## Urban accommodation

There are three major considerations when selecting a city hotel: room style, services needed and price. Choice of styles is between a Western-style ( *yōshitsu*) or Japanese-style (*washitsu*) room; *washitsu* rooms have *tatami* (grass-mat) floors and *futon* bedding instead of beds.

In any major city, the range of accommodation includes:
■ **First-class hotels** These fall into two distinct groups: deluxe hotels and chains, such as the Japanese chains Tōkyū and ANA, and Western chains such as Holiday Inn and Hilton. Location and status have a big bearing on price, as do front-desk services and the number of restaurants. All meals will be available, but none is included in the room price.
■ **Business hotels** These are usually conveniently located close to stations, have few front-desk services and the rooms are designed for single occupancy. The modest breakfast offered is the only meal available and is priced separately; the TVs are sometimes coin-operated. Space and amenities are reflected in the price.

Reservations are recommended at first-class hotels, particularly during holiday periods and, in Tōkyō, in January when hotels are particularly full of the families of students taking university-entrance examinations. Business hotels are correspondingly less busy during holidays.

## Provincial accommodation

If you are in search of the increasingly elusive 'real Japan', you may find something approaching it by trying one of these alternatives to conventional modern hotels:

■ **Traditional inns** *(ryokan)* In a true *ryokan*, style and service transcend business considerations. *Ryokan* are privately run, staffed by women and provide you with two meals (dinner and breakfast) in addition to your lodging. The food is Japanese, often served in your own Japanese-style room, where you sit, shoeless, on *tatami*-matted floors dressed in the *ryokan's yukata* and eat from a low table (still sitting on the floor). The same room is transformed into your bedroom at night, when the *futon* is laid out for you. Some *ryokan* will have communal baths and rooms with their own gardens; the term *ryokan* is sometimes misused, but price is generally a guide to whether or not you're getting the real thing. *Ryokan* can be found everywhere, the most prestigious being in and around Kyōto.

Is there a Japanese inn near here?
**Kono chikaku ni ryokan wa arimasu ka?**

hotel brochure

■ **Bed-and-breakfast** *(minshuku)* These are family-run bed-and-breakfast establishments where the food served is Japanese, the room style is *washitsu* and communication is largely in Japanese. *Minshuku* are economical, get you closer to the heart of Japanese domestic life and are a good bet in rural Japan.

■ **Pensions** *(penshon)* These are located in the provinces often near resorts, are run by couples who serve up Western food, frequently in homes which have a deliberate Western feel about them. Recommended when skiing or walking.

## Accommodation with a difference

There are several off-beat forms of accommodation which are inexpensive and fun precisely because they are so out of the ordinary. Among them are:

■ **Temple lodgings** *(shukubō)* Of interest if you want to experience the atmosphere of a Buddhist retreat, join in the meditation and eat traditional Japanese vegetarian cuisine. Kōya-san, outside Kyōto, is the largest and best known of these.

■ **Capsuleland** *(kapuseru hoteru)* Who else but the Japanese would even dream of modifying a shipping container to become a hotel room; *kapuseru* are not for the claustrophobic (nor women – these are strictly men only) nor are they really attractive for more than a short stay (you house your belongings in a locker). The novelty and price make them worth trying for a night or two.

■ **Love Hotels** (*rabu hoteru*) Gaudy theme hotels designed principally for meetings of a less business-like nature (the room tariff distinguishes between two-hour daytime or evening 'rests' and overnight 'stays'). These are mainly of interest to foreigners because the rates are low provided you check in after 10 pm and leave early to avoid 'rest' rates.

■ **Cycling Terminals** (*saikuringu hoteru*) Nothing odd here, just modestly priced cheap-and-cheerful accommodation located in the scenic areas any touring cyclist would be drawn to. A big plus is that you can hire cycles at these (as you can at railway stations and some hostels).

## Having a bath

Having a bath is not a simple matter in Japan (remember that this is the country where addresses begin with the postcode and empty taxis display a red light to solicit business). The main thing to remember is that you don't wash *in* the bath. You wash yourself clean *outside* the bath (shave, too, if you need to) before sliding gently in (bath water is customarily heated to 43°C). Bathing in Japan is about soaking, relaxing, socialising . . . even drinking if you wish.

*Onsen*, Japan's thermal spas, depend for their custom on the Japanese fondness for this transformation of a common ablution into an important social ritual. Many Japanese come to *ryokan* and *onsen* for this reason alone; in daily life, older Japanese still go to the local *sentō* (bath house) for a daily soak: men in the early morning and evening, women and older children at other times.

However, the Japanese love to see foreigners in *sentō* and are quick to tell you all the do's and don'ts of bathing. It's cheap, relaxing and a great way to meet people. A word of caution if you opt to take the plunge, particularly in a *sentō*: body tattoos, and earrings adorning male lobes and exotic female body parts do not yet enjoy the fashion status they have acquired in the West. Discretion is the better part of bathing diplomacy.

outdoor bath

# Phrasemaker

地図・ガイド

maps and guides

## Finding a place

| | |
|---|---|
| Is there a (Japanese inn/ B & B/hotel) near here? | **Kono chikaku ni (ryokan/ minshuku/hoteru) wa arimasu ka?** |
| Could I stay with a Japanese family? | **Hōmu sutei wa dekimasu ka?** |
| Do you have a (single/double/ twin/family/suite) room? | **(Shinguru/ Daburu/Tsuin/ Kazoku-beya/suiito) wa arimasu ka?** |
| Is it a (Western-style room/ Japanese-style room)? | **(Yōshitsu/Washitsu) desu ka?** |
| (One/Two) night(s), please. | **(Ippaku/Nihaku) onegai shimasu.** |
| one night, two days | **ippaku futsuka** |
| two nights, three days | **nihaku mikka** |
| one person | **hitori** |
| For (two people), please. | **(Futari) onegai shimasu.** |
| (two) adults, (one) child | **otona (futari), kodomo (hitori)** |
| May I see the room? | **Heya o mitemo ii desu ka?** |
| How much is it per night? | **Ippaku ikura desu ka?** |
| It is (small/expensive). | **(Semai/Takai) desu ne.** |
| Do you have anything (larger/ cheaper)? | **(Motto ōkii-no/Motto yasui-no) wa arimasu ka?** |
| That's fine. | **Kekkō desu.** |
| I'll take it. | **Sore de onegai shimasu.** |

| | |
|---|---|
| **Nanpaku desu ka?** | How many nights? |
| **Nanmei-sama desu ka?** | How many people? |
| **Mōshiwake gozaimasen, manshitsu de gozaimasu.** | I'm sorry, we're full. |
| **O-ko-sama wa hangaku de gozaimasu.** | It's half price for children. |

## Types of accommodation

| | |
|---|---|
| hotel | **hoteru** |
| business hotel | **bijinesu hoteru** |
| pension | **penshon** |
| youth hostel | **yūsu hosuteru** |
| campsite | **kyanpujō** |
| flat/apartment | **apāto** |
| lodging with a family | **hōmu sutei** |
| room | **heya** |
| Western-style room | **yōshitsu** |
| Japanese-style room | **washitsu** |
| Japanese inn | **ryokan** |
| Japanese B & B | **minshuku** |

## Specifications

| | |
|---|---|
| Is (breakfast/dinner) included? | **(Chōshoku/Yūshoku) tsuki desu ka?** |
| Does it come with a (bathroom/ shower/adjoining room)? | **(O-furo/Shawā/Tsuginoma) tsuki desu ka?** |
| Could I have a room with a (single/double) bed? | **(Shinguru /Daburu) beddo no aru heya o onegai shimasu.** |
| (quiet/large) room | **(shizukana/ōkii) heya** |
| a room with a view | **nagame no ii heya** |

| | |
|---|---|
| **(Chōshoku tsuki/Zeikomi) de gozaimasu.** | (Breakfast/Tax) is included. |

## Checking in

| | |
|---|---|
| I have a reservation in the name of (Smith). | **Yoyaku o shita (Sumisu) desu.** |
| Where can I park? | **Kuruma wa doko ni tomerare masu ka?** |
| Could you bring the luggage in. | **Nimotsu o hakonde kudasai.** |
| On which floor is the (room)? | **(Heya) wa nangai ni arimasu ka?** |

| | |
|---|---|
| **O-namae o (mōichido) onegai itashimasu.** | Your name (again), please. |
| **Kono yōshi ni go-kinyū kudasai.** | Please fill in this form. |
| **O-heya bangō wa . . . gōshitsu de gozaimasu.** | Your room number is . . . |
| **Kore ga o-heya no kii de gozaimasu.** | This is the key to your room. |
| **(Gokai) de gozaimasu.** | It's on the (fifth floor). |

## Services

| | |
|---|---|
| What time is (breakfast)? | **(Chōshoku) wa nanji desu ka?** |
| Is there (a lift/air conditioning)? | **(Erebētā/Eakon) wa arimasu ka?** |
| Do you have (a hair dryer/ an iron)? | **(Doraiyā/Airon) wa arimasu ka?** |
| Where is the (restaurant/bar)? | **(Resutoran/Bā) wa doko ni arimasu ka?** |
| Does the restaurant serve Japanese or Western dishes? | **Resutoran wa washoku desu ka yōshoku desu ka?** |
| How do I get an outside line from my room? | **Heya kara gaisen niwa dōyatte kakemasu ka?** |
| Do you offer a dry cleaning service? | **Dorai kuriiningu wa dekimasu ka?** |

| | |
|---|---|
| **(Shichiji) kara (jūji) made de gozaimasu.** | It's from (7am) to (10 am). |
| **(Sangai) ni gozaimasu.** | It's on the (third floor). |
| **'9' (kyū) o o-mawashi kudasai.** | Please dial '9'. |
| **Hai, gozaimsu.** | Yes, there (is/are). |
| **(Migite/Hidarite) ni gozaimasu.** | It's on your (right/left). |

## Amenities

| | |
|---|---|
| air conditioning | **eakon** |
| bathroom | **o-furo/basurūmu** |
| heating | **danbō** |
| minibar | **minibā** |
| room service | **rūmu sābisu** |
| shower | **shawā** |
| telephone | **denwa** |
| trouser press | **zubon puressā** |

entrance to men's bath

ボイラー室
BOILER ROOM

entrance to women's bath

## Problems

| | |
|---|---|
| The (door/key) doesn't work. | **(Doa/Kagi) ga kowarete imasu.** |
| There is a problem with the (telephone/air conditioning). | **(Denwā/Eakon) ga okashii desu.** |
| There is no (newspaper/soap). | **(Shinbun/Sekken) ga arimasen.** |
| There are no (blankets/pillows/slippers/towels). | **Heya ni (mōfu/makura/surippa/taoru) ga arimasen.** |
| I've locked myself out. | **Kagi o heya ni wasurete kite shimai mashita.** |
| I don't know how to operate the (shower/trouser press). | **(Shawā/Zubon puressā) no tsukaikata ga wakarimasen.** |
| How do you use the Japanese-style (bedding/toilets)? | **Nihonshiki no (futon/toire) wa dō tsukaimasu ka?** |

| | |
|---|---|
| alarm clock | **mezamashi dokei** |
| blinds | **buraindo** |
| light bulb | **denkyū** |
| door | **doa** |
| hair dryer | **doraiyā** |
| key/lock | **kii/kagi** |
| radio | **rajio** |
| shower | **shawā** |
| tap | **jaguchi** |
| telephone | **denwa** |
| television | **terebi** |

| | |
|---|---|
| **Sugu ni kakari no mono ga mairimasu/ukagaimasu.** | I'll send the person in charge right away. |
| **O-todoke itashimasu.** | I'll bring you some. |
| **O-shirabe itashimasu.** | I'll check it for you. |

## Asking for help and information

| | |
|---|---|
| Could I have a wake-up call at (7 am)? | **(Shichiji) ni mōningu kōru o onegai shimasu** |
| Is my dry cleaning ready? | **Kuriiningu wa dekite imasu ka?** |
| I would like to leave my (valuables) at the front desk. | **Furonto ni (kichōhin) o azuketain desu ga.** |
| Do you have a (town plan)? | **(Taun mappu) wa arimasu ka?** |
| Could you recommend (a restaurant). | **(Resutoran) o suisen shite kudasai.** |
| Would you order me a taxi, please. | **Takushii o yonde kudasai.** |

| | |
|---|---|
| **Hai, kashikomari mashita.** | Yes, certainly. |
| **Kore o dōzo.** | Here you are. |

## Hotel facilities

| | |
|---|---|
| bar | **bā** |
| bathroom | **o-furo** |
| outdoor bath | **rotenburo** |
| large communal bath | **dai yokujō** |
| central heating | **sentoraru hiitingu** |
| dining room (for private party) | **enkaijō** |
| fitness centre | **fittonesu sentā** |
| garden | **niwa** |
| hot spa | **onsen** |
| coin-operated laundry | **koin randorii** |
| public telephone | **kōshō denwa** |
| restaurant | **resutoran** |
| sauna | **sauna** |
| swimming pool | **pūru** |
| tennis court | **tenisu kōto** |

## Checking out

| | |
|---|---|
| What is the check-out time? | **Chekku auto wa nanji desu ka?** |
| I'd like to (check out/pay the bill), please. | **(Chekku auto/Shiharai) o onegai shimasu.** |
| How much is it in total? | **Zenbu de ikura desu ka?** |
| Do you take (credit cards/ traveller's cheques)? | **(Kādo/Toraberāzu chekku) wa tsukaemasu ka?** |
| By (cash/credit card/ traveller's cheques), please. | **(Genkin/Kādo/Toraberāzu chekku) de onegai shimasu.** |
| I think there is a mistake. | **Machigai ga arimasu.** |
| What's this charge for? | **Kono ryōkin wa nan desu ka?** |
| I haven't used the (minibar/ telephone). | **(Minibā/Denwa) wa tsukatte imasen.** |
| It's room (253). | **(Nihyaku gojū san) gōshitsu desu.** |

| | |
|---|---|
| **O-heya bangō o onegai shimasu.** | Your room number, please. |
| **(Minibā) wa o-tsukai ni narimashita ka?** | Have you used the (minibar)? |
| **(Koko ni) sain o onegai itashimasu.** | Sign (here), please. |

## Paying a bill

| | |
|---|---|
| tariff | **ryōkinhyō** |
| service charge | **sābisuryō** |
| tax | **zeikin** |
| parking charge | **chūsha ryōkin** |
| discount rate | **waribiki ryōkin** |
| excess charge/surcharge | **(chōka/warimashi) ryōkin** |
| telephone charge | **denwa ryōkin** |

## Language works

### Finding a place

**1** Making a reservation from a
Tourist Information Centre
- **Kono chikaku ni ryokan wa
arimasu ka?**
- **Hai. Nanmei-sama desu ka?**
- **Futari desu.**
- **Nanpaku desu ka?**
- **Nihaku onegai shimasu.**

What two questions are you asked?

ロイヤルパークホテル
**Royal Park Hotel**

### Checking in

**2** With a reservation
- **Yoyaku o shita Sumisu desu.**
- **Kono yōshi ni go-kinyū
kudasai. O-namae o mōichido
onegai itashimasu.**
- **Sumisu desu.**
- **O-heya bangō wa 253
gōshitsu de gozaimasu. Kore
ga o-heya no kii de
gozaimasu.**

The receptionist asks you two things.
One is to fill in a registration form.
What else?

### Services

**3** Asking about breakfast and
the telephone
- **Chōshoku wa nanji desu ka?**
- **Shichiji kara jūji made de
gozaimasu.**
- **Heya kara gaisen niwa
dōyatte kakemasu ka?**
- **Kyū o o-mawashi kudasai.**

Is breakfast between 7 and 10 am or
7 and 11 am?
What happens if you dial 'kyū'?

### Asking for help

**4** Going out to a restaurant
- **Sumimasen. Resutoran o
suisen shite kudasai.**
- **Hai, kashikomari mashita.
Kono resutoran ga yūmei
desu. Kore o dōzo.**
- **Takushii o yonde kudasai.**
- **Hai, kashikomari mashita.**
(**yūmei** = famous)

You ask the person who recommends
a restaurant to make a reservation for
you: true/false?

### Checking out

**5** Using a credit card
- **Chekku auto o onegai
shimasu. Kādo de onegai
shimasu.**
- **Hai, kashikomari mashita. O-
heya bangō o onegai
shimasu.**
- **Nihyaku gojū san gōshitsu
desu.**
- **Minibā wa o-tsukai ni
narimashita ka?**
- **Iie.**
- **Koko ni sain o onegai
itashimasu.**

The receptionist asks you two
questions. One is your room number.
What is the other question, to which
your answer is 'No'?

## Try it out

### Key words

What is the Japanese for these words?

1 hotel
2 youth hostel
3 television
4 restaurant
5 lodging with a family
6 air conditioning
7 coin-operated laundry
8 bathroom
9 key

### As if you were there

You arrive at a hotel to check in. Complete the dialogue below in Japanese.

- ☐ **Irasshaimase.**
- ■ (Say Good afternoon and explain that you have a reservation in the name of [your surname])
- ☐ **Kono yōshi ni go-kinyū kudasai. O-namae o mōichido onegai itashimasu. O-heya bangō wa 115 gōshitsu de gozaimasu.**
- ■ (Ask what time breakfast is)
- ☐ **Shichi-ji kara jūji made de gozaimasu.**
- ■ (Ask where the restaurant is)
- ☐ **Sangai ni gozaimasu. Kore ga o-heya no kii de gozaimasu.**
- ■ (Ask which floor the room is on)
- ☐ **Gokai de gozaimasu.**
- ■ (Ask if there is a lift)
- ☐ **Hai, gozaimasu. Migite ni gozaimasu.**
- ■ (Say thank you)

## Sound check

Japanese vowels are pure sounds and consistent in the way they are pronounced.
**a** as in **a**unt
**i** as in pol**i**ce
**u** as in c**u**pid
**e** as in **e**ffort
**o** as in **o**perator

**u** at the end of a sentence is often unpronounced.

Where you see a macron (–) over a vowel, lengthen the vowel sound when you pronounce it.
**Tōkyō** (Toh k'yoh); **Kyōto** (K'yoh to); **Ōsaka** (Oh sa ka).

'**ii**' is used instead of putting a macron over the vowel 'i'.

Long vowels change meanings:
**to** means 'door'
**tō** means 'ten'
**obasan** means 'aunt/woman'
**obāsan** means 'grandmother/old woman'

# Buying things

Japan is discernibly different to Hong Kong and Singapore when it comes to shopping. On the downside, prices are higher and,

with rare exceptions, like Akihabara (Tōkyō) or Ōsaka's Den-Den Town (Nipponbashi district), haggling is out of the question. On the other hand, choice is vast, quality consistently high, displays ingenious. For the financially challenged, browsing is a serious alternative to spending in consumer Japan.

Transactions are always in Yen – dollars are not accepted – and payment is by cash or plastic, but not cheque. When it comes to sizes, remember that Japan uses the metric system.

Shopping hours vary according to the type and size of outlet; be prepared for some inconsistency. Department stores are generally open from 10 am to 7 pm, six days a week; different *depāto* close one day a week Mondays–Thursdays, but there are always several open, and they are all open at weekends, with one exception. Supermarkets open seven days a week, generally from 9.30 am to 8 pm; smaller shops (other than boutiques) are the same, closing occasionally every few weeks. Because Japanese children go to school on Saturdays, Sunday is a big day for shopping, when many streets are turned into traffic-free pedestrian zones for the day.

❗ Which days of the week are you normally closed?
🔴 **Teikyūbi wa nanyōbi desu ka?**

## Shopping more cheaply

Duty-free shopping should not be confused with discounting, nor will the Japanese combine them. You will need your passport for duty-free purchases; duty-free shops such as LAOX clearly advertise themselves as such. Discounting is generally confined to particular markets, like second-hand cameras, or to particular areas, like Akihabara.

Store-wide sales throughout Japan generally take place in January and July; out-of-season sales, which are advertised in newspapers and foreign language tourist magazines, often take place in March and, to a lesser extent, September. Keep your eyes peeled in shops for sale bins, which permanently feature savings on Japanese-style tableware and nearly-past-its-sell-by-date film, which is normally very expensive in Japan.

Price differences between the big cities like Tōkyō or Ōsaka and small towns and cities are not great – 10% in general. If you prefer to shop in small local shops, do it for the local colour, not for the economics.

❗ How much is this one?
🔴 **Kore wa ikura desu ka?**

'100 yen' shop

## Specialities

There is such a vast range of **electronic gadgetry**, from audio to toys, that it is virtually impossible to visit Akihabara or Den-Den Town without spending. Big Camera in Ikebukuro or Yodobashi Camera in Shinjuku display the latest electronic cameraware. Less known is that Japanese recorded music (CDs and tapes) is of particularly high quality (Wave; Tower Records; Virgin; HMV).

## Shopping options

At the pinnacle of Japan's vast retail pyramid sit *depāto* or department stores. These offer a Total Shopping Experience, including art galleries, restaurants, cinemas plus a full range of consumer items. They also offer childcare facilities, gift advice centres, gift wrapping, special counters for unusually large (ie foreigners') sizes and overseas delivery services (Isetan and Seibu have the best reputations for this).

■ **Underground shopping malls** which lead into subway stations and boutique complexes like Laforet (Harajuku, Tōkyō) and Seed (Shibuya, Tōkyō) offer variety and enable you to head straight to the kind of goods you want. Names can be highly misleading: *Tōkyū Hands* is a DIY chain, *Printemps* is Japanese, not French, *Bingo-Ya* is a traditional craft bazaar. *Wakō* is so exclusive it can dare to close on Sundays.

■ **Flea markets** are good for antiques but usually open only on the first Sunday of the month, generally near shrines and stations (Tōgo-Jinja Shrine, Harajuku; Nogi Shrine, Akasaka).

■ **Traditional goods and crafts** – lacquerware, fine porcelain and pottery, pearls, fans and screens, wooden combs and dolls – are more accessible via flea markets, antique fairs (Tōkyō has three a year) and shopping complexes (Aoyama; Ginza).

If you intend giving anything you buy as a gift, try out the Tsutsumu Factory (*tsutsumu* literally means 'to wrap up') in Shibuya; it specialises exclusively in wrapping things.

❗ Could I have a receipt, please?
**Reshiito o onegai shimasu.**

designates some artists and craftsmen 'Living National Treasures', the cost of designer clothing or pottery thrown by a master is staggering.

## Food shopping

Though meat, rice and fruit prices are monstrously high, food shopping is interesting and varied. Supermarkets like *Meidi-Ya* cater for foreign tastes, *depāto* devote their (very large) basements to Japanese foods, their top floors to food and drink imports.

Rice, until recently sold only in speciality shops, can now be found even in DIY stores and petrol-station shops.

Tōkyō's Tsukiji district boasts the largest fish market in Asia, offering visitors early morning tours and fish breakfasts in nearby *sushi-ya*. Vending machines sell respectable convenience foods; don't leave Japan without trying a box lunch (*o-bentō*, see p66) available everywhere, particularly railway stations.

## Things to look for

Less obvious and more affordable gifts are handmade paper, woodblock prints and books, and kitchen knives and kites are great fun. Second-hand camera bodies and lenses are an exception to the Japanese obsession with the unique and the new.

## Things to avoid

Computers and software are, surprisingly, non-starters. Also, Japan's fashion and design genius has failed to reach footwear, with the exception of clogs (*geta*) and sandals (*zōri*). In a country which

open

# Phrasemaker

## Phrases to use anywhere

closed today

| | |
|---|---|
| I'm looking for . . . | . . . o sagashite imasu. |
| I'm looking for (picture postcards/ an English-language newspaper). | (Ehagaki/Eiji shinbun) o sagashite imasu. |
| What's the local speciality? | Koko no meibutsu wa nan desu ka? |
| this one | kore |
| that one | sore |
| that one over there | are |
| I'll take . . . | . . . ni shimasu. |
| How much is . . . ? | . . . wa ikura desu ka? |
| How much is it? | Kore wa ikura desu ka? |
| How much is it altogether? | Zenbu de ikura desu ka? |
| Do you take (Visa/Diner's Club)? | (Biza/Daināzu Kurabu) kādo wa tsukae masu ka? |
| Could I have a receipt, please? | Reshiito o onegai shimasu. |
| | |
| **Irasshaimase.** | May I help you? |
| **Nani o o-sagashi deshō ka?** | What are you looking for? |
| **Kore de gozaimasu.** | Here you are. |
| **Shōshō o-machi kudasai mase.** | Would you please wait a moment? |
| **Hoka ni nani ka?** | Anything else? |
| **Gōkei de (ichiman-en) de gozaimasu.** | That's (¥10,000) in total. |
| **Urikire de gozaimasu.** | We're sold out. |
| **Dōzo mata okoshi kudasai mase.** | Please come back again. |

## At the cash register

| | |
|---|---|
| **Irasshaimase.** | Welcome/May I help you? |
| **Kochira de yoroshii deshō ka?** | Is this everything? |
| **Gōkei de (¥16,000 = ichiman rokusen-en) de gozaimasu.** | Altogether, that comes to (¥16,000). |
| **Chōdo itadakimasu.** | That's just right (the exact amount). |
| **Kādo o o-azukari itashimasu.** | Your credit card – thank you. |
| **Koko ni sain o onegai itashimasu.** | Would you sign here, please. |
| **(¥4,000 = Yonsen-en) no o-tsuri de gozaimasu.** | Your change comes to (¥4,000). |
| **Reshiito no o-kaeshi de gozaimasu.** | Here is your receipt. |

(see p21 for numbers)

## Names of shops

| | |
|---|---|
| bakery | **pan-ya** |
| bank | **ginkō** |
| bookshop | **hon-ya** |
| chemists/pharmacy | **yakkyoku/kusuri-ya** |
| department store | **depāto** |
| electrical shop | **denki-ya** |
| kiosk | **kiosuku** |
| photo shop | **shashin-ya** |
| post office | **yūbinkyoku** |
| souvenir shop | **miyage hinten/o-miyage-ya** |

## At a department store

| | |
|---|---|
| On which floor are (electrical goods/kimonos)? | **(Denki seihin/Kimono) wa nangai ni arimasu ka?** |
| I'm looking for the (cashier/toilets). | **(Reji/Toire) o sagashite imasu.** |
| Would you gift-wrap this, please? | **Kore o purezento yō ni tsutsunde kudasai.** |
| gift/present | **gifuto/purezento** |
| wrapping | **rappingu** |
| bargain | **bāgen** |
| sale | **sēru** |

| | |
|---|---|
| roof floor | **RF/okujō** |
| fifth floor | **6F/rokkai** |
| fourth floor | **5F/gokai** |
| third floor | **4F/yonkai** |
| second floor | **3F/sangai** |
| first floor | **2F/nikai** |
| ground floor | **1F/ikkai** |
| basement | **BF/chikai** |

## Departments

案内所
Information

| | |
|---|---|
| department | **uriba** |
| accessories | **akusesarii** |
| bedding | **shingu** |
| clocks/watches | **tokei** |
| event hall | **moyooshimono kaijō** |
| foods | **shokuryōhin** |
| furniture | **kagu** |
| jewellery | **kikinzoku** |
| kimonos | **gofuku** |
| kitchen goods | **daidokoro yōhin** |
| ladies' wear | **fujinfuku** |
| men's wear | **shinshifuku** |
| restaurant | **resutoran** |

kimono shop

## At the information desk

| | |
|---|---|
| What time does the store (open/close)? | **(Kaiten/Heiten) wa nanji desu ka?** |
| Which days of the week are you normally closed? | **Teikyūbi wa nanyōbi desu ka?** |
| Do you have (stationery/restaurants)? | **(Bunbōgu/Resutoran) wa arimasu ka?** |
| **Heiten wa yoru no (hachiji) de gozaimasu.** | We close at (8 pm). |
| **Teikyūbi wa (Suiyōbi) de gozaimasu.** | We close on (Wednesdays). |
| **(Shokuryōhin/Kimono) wa (chikai/gokai) de gozaimasu.** | (Food is/Kimonos are) (in the basement/on the fifth floor). |
| **(Kamera) wa konokai ni gozaimasu.** | (Cameras) are on this floor. |
| **(Kochira/Achira) de gozaimasu.** | (This/That) way, please. |

| | |
|---|---|
| cashier/cash register/desk | **o-kaikei/reji** |
| entrance | **iriguchi** |
| exit | **deguchi** |
| lift | **erebētā** |
| escalator | **esukarētā** |

エレベーター

lift

## Buying clothes and footwear

| | |
|---|---|
| I'm just looking, thanks. | **Miteiru dake desu, dōmo.** |
| I'd like (pyjamas/ties/wooden clogs). | **(Pajama/Nekutai/Geta) ga hoshiin desu ga.** |
| May I try (it/them) on? | **Shichaku shitemo ii desu ka?** |
| It's a bit (big/small). | **Chotto (ōkii/chiisai) desu.** |
| I'm size (13). | **Watashi no saizu wa (jūsan) gō desu.** |
| What size is this? | **Saizu wa ikutsu desu ka?** |
| What's my shoe size? | **Watashi no kutsu no saizu wa ikutsu desu ka?** |
| May I see the size (11)? | **(Jūichi) gō saizu o misete kudasai.** |
| Do you have anything (bigger/smaller/cheaper)? | **Mō sukoshi (ōkii saizu/chiisai saizu/yasui) no wa arimasu ka?** |
| Do you have the same style in other colours? | **Kono irochigai wa arimasu ka?** |
| Do you have it in (black/green/red)? | **(Kuro/Midori/Aka) wa arimasu ka?** |
| This is fine. | **Chōdo ii desu.** |
| I like (it/them). | **Sore ga ii desu.** |
| I don't like (this/that) very much. | **(Kore/Sore) wa amari sukija arimasen.** |
| I'll take (this blouse/those socks). | **(Kono burausu/Sono sokkusu) ni shimasu.** |
| I'll think about it. | **Chotto kangaete mimasu.** |

(see p22 for colours)

## Clothes and footwear

| | |
|---|---|
| blouse | **burausu** |
| boot(s) | **būtsu** |
| cardigan | **kādigan** |
| jacket | **jaketto** |
| overcoat | **ōbā/kōto** |
| raincoat | **reinkōto** |
| shirt | **waishatsu** |
| shoe(s) | **kutsu** |
| sock(s) | **kutsushita/sokkusu** |
| suit | **sebiro/sūtsu** |
| sweater | **sētā** |
| tie | **nekutai** |
| (men's) trousers | **zubon** |
| (ladies') trousers | **pantsu** |
| wooden clog(s) | **geta** |

## Trying on clothes

| | |
|---|---|
| **Ikaga de gozaimasu ka?** | How do you like (it/them)? |
| **Kore wa (emu saizu/jūgo gō) de gozaimasu.** | This is a size (M/15). (M=medium) |
| **Saizu wa o-ikutsu de gozaimasu ka?** | What size do you take? |
| **(Nijūroku=26) senchi gurai kato omoimasu.** | About (26) cm, I think. |

## Food shopping

| | |
|---|---|
| How much (is it/are they) a kilo? | **Ichikiro ikura desu ka?** |
| (200) grams of this (ham/ potato) salad, please. | **Kono (hamu/poteto) sarada o (nihyaku) guramu kudasai.** |
| May I try some? | **Shishoku shite ii desu ka?** |
| How much is it for one bag? | **Hitofukuro ikura desu ka?** |
| A bag of these (rice crackers/ chestnuts), please. | **Kono (o-senbei/kuri) o hito- fukuro kudasai.** |
| A little more, please. | **Mō sukoshi onegai shimasu.** |
| That's fine. | **Sore de kekkō desu.** |

| | |
|---|---|
| a bottle/jar of . . . | **. . . ippon/hitobin** |
| a box of . . . | **. . . hitohako** |
| a slice of . . . | **. . . ichimai** |
| a tin of . . . | **. . . hitokan** |

(see p108–109 for counting terms)

| | |
|---|---|
| **Dore gurai sashiage masu ka?** | How much would you like? |
| **Kore de (ii/yoroshii) deshō ka?** | Is this (OK/fine) with you? |

## Fruits

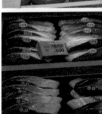

| | |
|---|---|
| fruit | **furūtsu** |
| apple | **ringo** |
| apricot | **anzu** |
| banana | **banana** |
| grape | **budō** |
| melon | **meron** |
| orange | **orenji** |
| peach | **momo** |
| pear | **nashi** |
| persimmon | **kaki** |
| pineapple | **painappuru** |
| satsuma | **mikan** |
| strawberry | **ichigo** |

## Vegetables

| | |
|---|---|
| asparagus | **asuparagasu** |
| broccoli | **burokkorii** |
| cabbage | **kyabetsu** |
| carrot | **ninjin** |
| cauliflower | **karifurawā** |
| celery | **serori** |
| cucumber | **kyūri** |
| green pepper | **piiman** |
| leek | **negi** |
| lettuce | **retasu** |
| mushroom | **masshurūmu** |
| onion | **tamanegi** |
| pea | **guriin piisu** |
| potato | **jagaimo/poteto** |
| spinach | **hōrensō** |
| sweet corn/maize | **tōmorokoshi** |
| tomato | **tomato** |

## Useful weights and measures

| | |
|---|---|
| gram (g) | **guramu** |
| kilo (kg) | **kiro guramu/kiro** |
| centilitres (cc) | **shii shii** |
| millilitres (ml) | **miri rittoru/miri rittā** |
| litres (l) | **rittoru/rittā** |
| millimetres (mm) | **miri mētoru/miri** |
| centimetres (cm) | **senchimētoru/senchi** |
| metres (m) | **mētoru** |

rice shop

photography shop

## Photography

| | |
|---|---|
| This one (= film), please. | **Kore o onegai shimasu.** |
| When will it be ready? | **Itsu dekimasu ka?** |
| Could I have it by (this afternoon/tomorrow morning)? | **(Gogo/Asu no asa) made ni deki masu ka?** |
| Do you have these batteries? | **Kono denchi wa arimasu ka?** |
| Could I have a film for (prints/slides)? | **(Purinto/Suraido) yō no fuirumu o kudasai.** |

| | |
|---|---|
| **O-namae o onegai shimasu?** | May I have your name, please? |
| **(Gogo/Ashita/Ashita no asa) made ni dekimasu.** | It will be ready by (the afternoon/ tomorrow/tomorrow morning). |

## At the post office

| | |
|---|---|
| I'd like to send this to (the UK/ the USA/France/Germany), please. | **Kore o (Igirisu/Amerika/ Furansu/Doitsu) ni okuritain desu ga.** |
| How much is it to send a postcard to (the UK/Australia)? | **(Igirisu/Ōsutoraria) made hagaki wa ikura desu ka?** |
| How much is it by (air/sea)? | **(Kōkūbin/Funabin) de ikura desu ka?** |
| How many days does it take? | **Nannichi gurai kakarimasu ka?** |
| One (¥70) stamp, please. | **(Nanajū-en) kitte o ichimai kudasai.** |
| I'd like to send this parcel 'express'. | **Kono kozutsumi o 'sokutatsu' de okuritain desu ga.** |

| | |
|---|---|
| **(Igirisu eno) hagaki wa (nanajū-en) desu.** | A postcard (to the UK) is (¥70). |
| **Kōkūbin de (nanajū-en) desu.** | It's (¥70) by air mail. |
| **(Amerika/Yōroppa) eno fūsho wa (nijūgo guramu) made . . . desu.** | A letter of up to (25g) to (the USA/Europe) is . . . |
| **Kono yōshi ni go-kinyū kudasai.** | Please fill in this form. |

## Postal terms

| | |
|---|---|
| aerogramme | **kōkū shokan** |
| express mail/first class | **sokutatsu** |
| letter | **fūsho/tegami** |
| parcel | **kozutsumi** |
| picture postcard | **ehagaki** |
| postcard | **hagaki** |
| stamp | **kitte** |

## Language works

## Phrases to use anywhere

**1** Buying an English newspaper
- □ **Irasshaimase.**
- ■ **Eiji shinbun o sagashite imasu.**
- □ **Kore de gozaimasu.**
- ■ **Kore wa ikura desu ka?**
- □ **Nihyaku-en de gozaimasu.**

Do they have English newspapers?
How much is the newspaper?

## At the information desk of a department store

**2** Asking about the opening and closing time
- □ **Heiten wa nanji desu ka?**
- ■ **Heiten wa yoru no hachiji de gozaimasu.**
- □ **Kimono wa nangai ni arimasu ka?**
- ■ **Kimono wa gokai de gozaimasu.**

What time does this department store close?
Which floor would you go to buy a kimono?

## Buying clothes and footwear

**3** Sold out?
- □ **Nani o o-sagashi deshō ka?**
- ■ **Jūichi gō saizu o misete kudasai.**
- □ **Hai. Kore de gozaimasu.**
- ■ **Midori wa arimasu ka?**
- □ **Urikire de gozaimasu.**

You got the size you wanted: true/false?
You got the colour you wanted: true/false?

**4** Big or small?
- □ **Saizu wa ikutsu desu ka?**
- ■ **Kore wa emu saizu de gozaimasu.**
- □ **Shichaku shitemo ii desu ka?**
- ■ **Hai. Dōzo kochira e.**

- ■ **Ikaga de gozaimasu ka?**
- □ **Mō sukoshi ōkii saizu no wa arimasu ka?**
- ■ **Shōshō o-machi kudasai mase.**

(**Dōzo kochira e.** = This way, please.)

You tried on a size 'M': true/false?
It was big enough for you: true/false?

## Food shopping

**5** Buying some rice crackers
- □ **Hitofukuro ikura desu ka?**
- ■ **Gohyaku-en de gozaimasu.**
- □ **O-senbei o hitofukuro kudasai.**

Is it ¥500 for one bag or two bags of rice crackers?

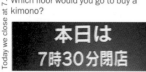

本日は
7時30分閉店

*Today we close at 7.30*

## Photography

**6** You have a film to be developed by the afternoon
- □ **Kore o onegai shimasu. Itsu dekimasu ka?**
- ■ **Ashita no gogo made ni dekimasu.**

When will the photographs be ready?

camera

## Buying at the post office

**7** You have a postcard and a parcel to send
- □ **Igirisu made hagaki wa ikura desu ka? Kōkūbin de onegai shimasu.**
- ■ **Igirisu eno hagaki wa nanajū-en desu.**
- □ **Kono kozutsumi o sokutatsu de okuritain desu ga.**
- ■ **Kono yōshi ni go-kinyū kudasai.**

How much is it to send a postcard by air mail to the UK?
What did the clerk ask you to do to send your parcel?

## Try it out

### Going shopping

Here is a shopping list. Ask the shop assistant for what you need.
- a kurisumasu kādo (nitsū)
- b fuirumu (nihon)
- c batterii (sanko)
- d ¥70 kitte (yonmai)
- e kōkū shokan (rokutsū)
- f ichigo (hitohako)
- g hamu (nihyaku guramu)

## Sound check

There are not very many Japanese consonants and, with the exception of the **n** sound, they are always pronounced in combination with a vowel. The basic consonant sounds are **k, s, t, h, m, y, r** and **w**. For example:
**ka** as in **kagi** (key)
**ki** as in **kimono**
**ku** as in **kuruma** (car)
**ke** as in **kekkon** (wedding)
**ko** as in **kore** (this)

# Café life

Drinking culture in Japan emphasizes the group and provides a safety valve for the frustrations and tensions which tend to build up in the repressed environment of a Japanese office. *Mizu shōbai* (the euphemistically named 'water trade') adds the lubricant for social interaction, providing both a basis and a *kimochi* (ambience) for all-important networking. Drinking is serious business in Japan; attitudes to alcohol are laid back. The Japanese are not legendary for their capacity for drink, due, it is said, to their low fat-weight ratios and a missing enzyme in their biochemistry. Whatever the reason, the Japanese are likely to get merry quicker than their Western counterparts. *Kanpai* (cheers!) literally means 'empty glass'; try to remember that for a Japanese host, your empty glass is a black mark on his hospitality. Consider the implications of all of this when planning a night out.

## Drinks

Japan's pronounced seasonality means that there are seasons for cold and hot drinks alike. Japan's summers are so hot and humid that you will need to drink lots of fluids throughout the day; the vending-machine industry makes this easy (there is even a vending machine on the summit of Mount Fuji), whether your tipple is a soft drink, iced tea or beer (the tinned hot coffee from vending machines is not recommended unless you wear

asbestos gloves). Here are some of the choices on offer:

### Alcoholic

Unless the drink is mixed, the etiquette is to pour for others and allow them to pour for you, raising your glass for the purpose and in thanks, pushing it towards the neck of the bottle as a non-verbal signal when no more is wanted. There is no gender-bias regarding drinking in Japan – Japanese men tolerate women imbibing just as much as Japanese society tolerates male inebriation.

■ **sake** A semi-mystical fermented rice wine (it's used in Shintō rites), said to be the world's most complex alcoholic drink (it combines some 400 tastes), served either cold *(reishu/hiyazake)* or warmed *(atsukan/nurukan)*, depending on the season (though unfortunately sometimes also to mask the flavour of nasty additives). Quality sake *(tokkyū* is the highest of three grades, but *jizake* is the purest – the sake equivalent of single malt whisky) is very smooth and appealing, unlike the hangover which awaits anyone underestimating its punch (four times the strength of beer). Taste grades range from -3, which is sweet, to +10, which is super dry (dryer = stronger).

traditional brazier

56

■ **shōchū** Sometimes referred to as the 'moonshine' or *eau de vie* of Japan, *shōchū* originally was rough, strong and sourced in the countryside, distilled from sweet potatoes or rice (if anyone tells you that it was originally a rural disinfectant, don't believe them!). Drinks manufacturers have hijacked the name to produce a tamer commercial version which can be mixed and is targeted at young professional women.

■ **umeshu** Sweet plum wine, a Japanese variation on sherry, good as an aperitif served over ice.

■ **biiru** German-style lager which has evolved into varieties like 'dry' and 'super-dry'. Draft beer *(nama biiru)* is particularly good, helped by intense competition between the four main brewers Kirin, Sapporo, Suntory and Asahi, in general order of popularity. Try to remember that *biru* means building in Japanese.

■ **mizuwari** Whisky and water, made from an indigenous blended whisky. It's mixed at a strength of approximately one part whisky to five parts water, and looks like weak tea.

### Non-alcoholic

■ **Pocari Sweat** You really can't travel all

the way to Japan and not try it. It's an innocuously pleasant isotonic drink whose mere name will enliven your tales when you relive your trip back home.

■ **Calpis** A light, yoghurt-based drink.

■ **Jolt** Sadistically created for caffeine freaks.

■ Health drinks like carrot juice have become fashionable as more professional women enter the labour force, the idea pushed by drinks manufacturers being that these replace the energy lost in the daily struggle of today's corporate warriors.

■ **cha** Generic term for tea, of which there are numerous varieties depending on where you are and the temperature. *O-cha* refers to standard green tea (green because, unlike Western tea, the tea leaves are not roasted) served to visitors in offices and homes as well as in restaurants. As with all teas in Japan, you don't add lemon, sugar or milk. If you like it, why not try *o-cha* flavoured ice-cream (which, not surprisingly, is unique to Japan). Another variety, *mugi-cha* is buckwheat tea, particularly refreshing served iced.

## Places to drink

The prodigous number of drinking outlets found throughout Japan is matched by enormous variety in both size and type of establishment. Lager *biiru* is the dominant alcoholic drink in Japan, generally served alongside sake, *shōchū* and whisky in the following watering holes:

■ **akachōchin** Identifiable by the red lanterns hanging outside, these basic Japanese-style pubs serve mainly beer and sake along with simple foods to Japanese working men. Smoky and male-oriented but cheap, cheerful and generally neither overcrowded nor ear-splittingly noisy.

making these a good place for you to sample life as the average Japanese lives it.

■ **kakuteru bā** Smart, stylish and pricey, with an emphasis on spirits and mixed drinks.

■ **karaoke bā** *kara* means 'empty', *oke* is a Japanese abbreviation for orchestra – you provide the vocals, the bar provides the BGM (background music) and the lyrics on a screen (in case you try to weasel out that way). In these sing-along bars, peer pressure ensures that you can't avoid your turn at the microphone, as your group cheers you on.

■ **raunji bā** Less stylish than cocktail bars, more for informal meetings amidst the background piano *musak*. Visiting foreigners may care to try the *sukai raunji* (sky lounge bars) found on top of the big hotels and office buildings, particularly after nightfall.

■ **wain bā** Trendy wine bars popular with young professionals. Not cheap, but generally less noisy, crowded, smoke filled and male oriented.

Women need to exercise some care in choosing where they drink. Karaoke bars, lounges, hotel and wine bars welcome men and women; the rest are male preserves where women will either feel – or be made to feel – out of place.

■ **bā/kurabu** Hostess bars where you pay handsomely for having your drink poured by a woman who is not your wife, partner or girlfriend. Often found behind closed doors and off-limits to foreigners (if you look like you can't or won't pay the bill at the end of the evening). A phenomenon of the *shayōzoku* (expense account brigade) culture, with their soft lighting and music, they are a generally harmless executive ego-tickle best avoided by visitors – except as an honoured guest.

■ **biyagāden** Roof-top beer gardens are opened by *depāto* and large office buildings when the weather gets hot. They are enjoyable provided you can tolerate the noise and crowds, especially office parties with their inevitable tipsy *sarariiman*.

■ **gaijin bā** Bars specialising in foreign themes and drinks, often without cover charges. Fine if you need to touch homebase culturally, though watch out for Japanese wanting to practise their English; not the best place to discover Japan as it really is.

■ **ippai nomiya/izakaya** Much more the real Japan. Small, boozy and boisterous, the range of drinks is limited, and menus are likely to be only in Japanese. The reasonable prices attract a younger crowd,

# Phrasemaker

## Asking what there is

| | |
|---|---|
| Do you have . . . ? | **. . . wa arimasu ka?** |
| Do you have any (sandwiches/cakes)? | **(Sandoitch/Kēki) wa arimasu ka?** |
| Do you have (coke/grapefruit juice)? | **(Kōra/Gurēpufurūtsu jūsu) wa arimasu ka?** |
| What (soft drinks/hot drinks) do you have? | **(Sofuto dorinku/Atatakai nomimono) wa nani ga arimasu ka?** |

## Coffee shops

| | |
|---|---|
| **kafe** | café |
| **kissaten** | generic term for a coffee shop/tea room |
| **kōhii shoppu** | coffee shop |
| **tii rūmu** | tea room |
| **wafū kissa** | Japanese-style coffee shop/tea room |

## Drinks

| | |
|---|---|
| something to drink | **nomimono** |
| soft drink | **sofuto dorinku** |
| juice | **jūsu** |
| cola | **kōra** |
| ginger ale | **jinjaēru** |
| ice-cream with soda water | **kuriimu sōda** |

| | |
|---|---|
| cold drink | **tsumetai nomimono** |
| iced coffee | **aisu (kōhii)** |
| iced tea | **aisu tii** |
| iced cocoa | **aisu kokoa** |
| iced milk | **aisu miruku** |

| | |
|---|---|
| hot drink | **hotto dorinku** |
| coffee | **hotto (kōhii)** |
| decaffeinated coffee | **kafeinresu kōhii** |
| milky tea | **miruku tii** |
| lemon tea | **remon tii** |
| hot chocolate | **hotto chokorēto/kokoa** |
| hot milk | **hotto miruku** |
| cappuccino | **kapuchiino** |
| (Japanese) green tea | **o-cha/Nihoncha** |

| | |
|---|---|
| fruit juice | **furūtsu jūsu** |
| apple juice | **appuru jūsu** |

| | |
|---|---|
| banana juice | **banana jūsu** |
| blueberry juice | **burūberii jūsu** |
| grape juice | **gurēpu jūsu** |
| melon juice | **meron jūsu** |
| orange juice | **orenji jūsu** |
| tomato juice | **tomato jūsu** |

| | |
|---|---|
| alcohol | **arukōru** |
| beer | **biiru** |
| domestic (Japanese) beer | **kokusan biiru** |
| draft beer | **nama biiru** |
| imported beer | **yunyū biiru** |
| brandy | **burandē** |
| campari and soda | **kanpari sōda** |
| gin and tonic | **jin tonikku** |
| liqueur | **rikyūru** |
| plum wine | **umeshu** |
| red wine | **aka wain** |
| white wine | **shiro wain** |
| rosé | **roze (wain)** |
| sparkling wine | **supākuringu wain** |
| (Japanese) sake | **(Nihonshu) o-sake** |
| unheated sake | **reishu/hiyazake** |
| traditional distilled spirit | **shōchū** |
| whisky | **uisukii** |

## Snacks

| | |
|---|---|
| something to eat | **tabemono** |
| cheese sandwich | **chiizu sando(itch)** |
| crêpe | **kurēpu** |
| ham sandwich | **hamu sando(itch)** |
| hot dog | **hotto doggu** |
| ice-cream | **aisukuriimu** |
| American-style pancake | **hottokēkii** |
| sandwich | **sandoitchi** |
| sorbet | **shābetto** |
| toast | **tōsuto** |

## Bars

| | |
|---|---|
| **biyagāden** | beer garden |
| **wain bā** | wine bar |
| **karaoke bā** | bar equipped for karaoke |
| **bā/kurabu/sunakku** | bar/club/snack bar |
| **kakuteru ba/raunji bā** | cocktail bar/lounge bar |
| (stylish, normally located on the top floor of major hotels and sky scrapers) | |
| **izakaya** | Japanese style pub |
| **akachōchin** | 'red lantern' |
| **(ippai) nomiya** | '(one-drink) watering hole' |

## Containers

| | |
|---|---|
| big mug for drinking beer | **jokkii** |
| bottle | **botoru** |
| ceramic sake carafe | **tokkuri** |
| coffee cup | **kōhii kappu** |
| glass (for alcohol) | **gurasu** |
| glass (for water) | **koppu** |
| half bottle | **hāfu botoru** |
| tea cup | **tii kappu** |
| tiny cup for sake | **sakazuki** |

| | |
|---|---|
| **Nani ni nasai masu ka?** | What would you like? |
| **Mōshiwake gozaimasen.** | I'm sorry. |
| **Shinagire de gozaimasu.** | We've run out. |

## Ordering

| | |
|---|---|
| I'll have (an egg sandwich/ a pancake), please. | **(Tamago sando/ Hotto kēki) o kudasai.** |
| Could I have (a coffee/an orange juice), please. | **(Kōhii/Orenji jūsu) o onegai shimasu.** |
| A (table d'hôte breakfast/ lunch), please. | **(Mōningu setto/Ranchi setto) o kudasai.** |
| (This one/That one/ That one over there), please. | **(Kore/Sore/Are) kudasai.** |

| | |
|---|---|
| **O-kimari (desu/deshō) ka?** | Are you ready to order? |
| **(Koori/Remon) wa iremasu ka?** | With (ice/lemon)? |
| **Dochira (desu/deshō) ka?** | Which one? |
| **Serufu sābisu desu.** | It's self-sevice. |
| **(Miruku/O-satō/Supūn) wa kochira desu/de gozaimasu.** | (Milk/Sugar/Spoons) is/are here. |
| **Dōzo.** | Here you are. |
| **O-shiharai wa reji de (onegai shimasu/itashimasu).** | Please pay at the till. |

## Others

| | |
|---|---|
| Can you give me a few more minutes? | **Mō ni sanpun matte kudasai.** |
| How much is it? | **Ikura desu ka?** |
| Is there a (telephone)? | **(Denwa) wa arimasu ka?** |
| Where are the (toilets), please? | **(Toire) wa doko desu ka?** |

ice-cream

## Snack time

Using the instructions below, make the appropriate choice from this menu.
(**to** = and)

| | |
|---|---|
| Hotto doggu | ¥350 |
| Jin tonikku | ¥850 |
| Kurēpu | ¥400 |
| Orenji jūsu | ¥800 |
| Tōsuto | ¥380 |
| Kapuchiino | ¥500 |
| Hotto kēki | ¥550 |
| Hotto chokorēto | ¥480 |
| Kōhii | ¥450 |
| Kōra | ¥350 |
| Jinjaēru | ¥350 |

## Language works

**1** Asking what there is
☐ **Sandoitch wa arimasu ka?**
■ **Tamago sando, chiizu sando, hamu sando ga gozaimasu.**
☐ **Atatakai nomimono wa nani ga arimasu ka?**
■ **Hotto kōhii, tii, hotto chokorēto ga gozaimasu.**

What three kinds of sandwich and hot drinks do they serve?

a a pancake and a hot drink which together cost ¥1,000
b any snack plus a glass of juice which cost a total of ¥1,200
c **Gohyaku-en no nomimono to sanbyaku hachijū-en no tabemono**
d **Arukōru to sanbyaku gojū-en no tabemono**

## Ordering

**2** Needing more time to decide what to have
☐ **O-kimari desu ka?**
■ **Mō ni, sanpun matte kudasai.**
. . .
☐ **Nani ni nasai masu ka?**
■ **Kore kudasai.**
☐ **Dochira desu ka?**
■ **Kore desu . . . 'Umeshu'.**

You order something to drink: true/false?

## Ordering

**3** Self-service
☐ **Kore kudasai.**
■ **Serufu sābisu desu. O-shiharai wa reji de onegai shimasu.**

Where are you asked to pay?

Tasty coffee, please

## Where to go?

What kind of bar is most appropriate for each of the situations described here?

a   A romantic place to enjoy a quiet evening with your partner.
b   On a hot summer's day, an open-air establishment where you can enjoy a Japanese lager such as 'Kirin' or 'Sapporo'.
c   Somewhere you can go with friends to snack, drink and sing.

**karaoke bā**
**izakaya**
**biya gāden**
**kakuteru bā/raunji bā**
**akachōchin**
**(ippai) nomiya**

Some consonant sounds common in other languages are missing altogether in Japanese. For example:

l and r   instead of two distinct sounds, in Japanese there is a single sound which falls between the English **l** and **r** sounds, arguably closer to the **l** sound, as in **Hiroshi** (a man's given name) or **daruma** (a papier-mâché doll)

v   the **b** sound is used instead of **v**. 'Avec' in Japanese becomes **abekku**

f/ph   a soft **hu** sound is used instead. **Fuji-san** (Mount Fuji) is actually said **Hu/ji/sa/n**

# Eating out

The popular image of Japanese cuisine is its emphasis on presentation, its healthy, low-fat nature and its exotic – even weird (depending on what your norm is) – character. Overlooked in these stereotypes is the central importance which food and drink have in Japanese life and the qualities which lie behind the artistic presentation of dishes: the freshness and quality of ingredients, the ingenuity which has spawned a huge variety of different dishes, the skill and training of chefs.

tofu dishes

## When to eat

There is a staggering number of restaurants and coffee shops serving food throughout the day, including breakfast, which is generally not included in the price of your room (*ryokan* excepted). The long hours and long commuting distances faced by *sarariiman* (Japanese businessmen), along with the emphasis on business socializing, means that there simply have to be enormous numbers of places where you can eat out.

kaiten zushiya

Lunch is taken early (about midday) and quickly (30–45 minutes); it is not the social (nor alcoholic) event generally associated with business entertaining; this takes place in the evening among professionals, unaccompanied by spouses.

The Japanese eat dinner relatively early too; this allows them to go on to other haunts for *nijikai* (see p107) where the emphasis shifts to drinking. Bars, clubs and restaurants in urban Japan thin out as the time of the last train to the suburbs approaches; this explains why you may be 'strap-hanging' on the underground at 11 pm.

## Where to eat

Meals out are a good buy in Japan, particularly if you avoid Western and fast-food restaurants. At the lower end of the scale, around all railway stations, you will find noodle shops where you can eat at the counter or even standing up; these areas are also a good source of *o-bentō* (see p66).

For modestly priced sit-down meals (*setto* and *teishoku* or set menus offer the best value), underground shopping malls and department stores have dozens of small restaurants (these areas are known as *resutoran gai* – 'restaurant street') which cater for office workers, many displaying *sanpuru* (plastic models of the dishes on offer, with prices displayed alongside) outside. If you

Set course meal for two ¥650

定食
営業時間
AM11ᵗ–PM2
650円

exquisitely decorated private dining rooms (discretion is all) usually overlooking classical Japanese gardens, not forgetting the company of a professional dinner companion. *Ryōtei* are sometimes found in what the Japanese call *karyūkai* – flower and willow worlds – of which there are seven in Tōkyō alone.

are browsing in a *depāto*, a glance at the upper-floor plans will reveal numerous restaurants - keep to Japanese for the best value.

In smaller towns or in *shitamachi* neighbourhoods, *yakitori-ya*, *okonomiyaki-ya*, *sushi-ya* (some with revolving counters – *kaiten zushi* – serving varied sushi plates on a miniaturised airport baggage carousel) and *tenpura-ya* uniformly offer a very Japanese ambience, good food and an opportunity to practise your Japanese. If they shout *irasshaimase* (welcome!) as you walk in the door, you know you're in the right place.

You may want to precede your meal with a stop at an *akachōchin* (Japanese pub), denoted by the red paper lantern outside, where savouries like aubergine sautéed in sesame paste are served with the beer. After a meal, you may not like the prices of the coffee served in *kōhii shoppu* (coffee shops) but the atmosphere is pleasant, unhurried and tranquil, and the desserts are a calorie-rich bonus.

At the top end, the best value comes from restaurants famous for their cuisine alone; status imposes astronomical costs in Japan. If you are prepared to part with ¥70,000 per head, the place to do it is in a quintessentially Japanese restaurant known as a *ryōtei*. *Ryōtei* feature

## Don't miss

- **yakitori** Japanese kebabs of all kinds – vegetables, meat (particularly chicken) – barbecued over a charcoal fire on bamboo skewers, after first being dipped in or basted with a sweetened soy-based barbecue sauce.
- **teppan yaki** Griddle cooking in which you sit around a large griddle, possibly in the company of strangers, while a chef grills meat (beef or pork), fish and/or vegetables of your choice in front of you in a blaze of frenzied cutting and food flipping which is a vital part of the experience.
- **sukiyaki** Vegetables, *shirataki* (shredded devil's tongue root), *tōfu* and thinly sliced beef cooked at your table in a large iron pan in a broth of soy sauce and sweet rice wine, after which those dining together select what they want from the pot and dip them in individual bowls of raw egg before eating. A variation on this is called *nabemono*, a Japanese version of a stockpot, cooked in either a ceramic casserole or an iron pot. (For *sumō* versions, *chanko nabe*, see p81.)

■ **shabu-shabu** A dish similar to *sukiyaki*; vegetables (mushrooms, Chinese leaves, spring onions, spring chrysanthemums) and cooked slivers of beef in a stock-based soup. The pieces you select are then dipped in a variety of sauces (soy, lemon juice, *miso*, sesame) and sometimes finished off with noodles, which are added directly to any remaining soup.

■ **sushi and sashimi** Raw fish; *sushi* is served on a bed of vinegared rice with horseradish and eaten with a soy dipping sauce followed by pickled ginger; *sashimi* is raw fish pieces eaten with a dipping sauce which contains *wasabi* (very hot, green horseradish). *Fugu sashi* (globefish) is a particular favourite of some Japanese because parts of it are toxic (the potential danger is a thrill) and for a few customers every year, fatal.

o-bentō shop

■ **soba/udon/rāmen** Japanese pasta. *Soba* (buckwheat noodles) is associated with Tōkyō cuisine and eaten cold (*zaru soba*) in the summer or served hot in a soup with king prawn and vegetable tempura. *Udon*, associated with Osaka cuisine, is a thick, white noodle most often served in a soup with vegetables. *Rāmen* is a thin, white Chinese noodle served in soup with vegetables and/or meat. It's a quick and cheap meal if you're pressed for time and is immortalised in Itami Juzo's popular film, *Tanpopo*.

■ **tenpura** Vegetables and fish battered in wheat flour and egg and deep-fried into a kind of savoury fritter, eaten hot after being dipped into soy sauce seasoned with fish stock, sweet rice wine and grated white radish. Can be eaten by the piece in a specialist *tenpura-ya* or as part of a set meal elsewhere.

■ **okonomiyaki** The Japanese will tell you it's their version of a pizza; in fact it's more like a *Kansai* version of a Spanish omelette (a Japanese omelette (*tamagoyaki*), being quite unlike anything made with eggs in the West). The wheat base is made from a spicy batter topped with your choice of meat, seafood, vegetables, even egg; this is then cooked on a hotplate at your table (you can do it yourself, which is why it's inexpensive) and topped with a thick, piquant sauce.

bentō

■ **o-bentō** Box lunches which contain something pickled, grilled or fried and boiled including *tenpura* pieces, grilled fish, several pieces of *sushi* or *sashimi*, boiled rice and various pickles. The ingredients, quantity and quality vary with the seasons, the region where the *o-bentō* is made and the price paid; always found in and around railway stations, ports and airports. The term literally means 'convenient'; *o-bentō* are pre-cooked in the mornings and often eaten by travellers since they are pre-packed in compartmentalised boxes and require no further preparation.

*Tabehōdai* is Japan's version of 'all you can eat for ¥xxx', often available with *shabu-shabu* and *yakiniku* ('grill it yourself'). Good value when you're really hungry.

# Alternative cuisine

There are several items that are likely to crop up on a Japanese menu which, although perfectly normal to the Japanese, are decidedly unusual to Westerners. Two of the most common are *gobō* (burdock) and *hasu* (lotus). Burdock is a fibrous, rather tasteless brown root vegetable which is cooked in a soya broth to give it flavour and served in thinly sliced strips as an accompaniment to other dishes. Lotus is another rather insipid root vegetable; it's white with a 'holey' texture and is grown in ponds. Despite this unappetising start, by the time it has been cooked in soya broth and served cut into round pieces as an accompaniment it is very tasty.

Saying *saishokushugi-sha desu* ('I'm vegetarian') tends to ring alarm bells in the minds of most Japanese hosts mainly because they don't really know what this implies for what you will or won't eat; despite Japan's Buddhist tradition, the modern notion of vegetarianism is still relatively unknown and accordingly there is little specific provision in the way of specialised vegetarian restaurants or vegetarian dishes and menus flagged in other restaurants. Wholefoods and macrobiotic dishes

are only now becoming fashionable in Tōkyō *depāto*. That said, you will have few problems in finding dishes suitable for vegetarians – it is simply a case of recognising the non-meat dishes. You can usually choose from conventional Japanese menus and get very close to a full vegan meal: tofu comes in soup, steak, salad, vegetable and sweet forms. With some set menus, there may be some meat included, but you can simply avoid these dishes and eat only the vegetarian ones. *Makizushi* is a Japanese equivalent of a sandwich: vinegared rice balls wrapped in dried seaweed; *kappa maki* is similar, a vegetarian form of sushi with cucumber or pickles in place of fish. You can have a vegetarian *o-bentō* provided you order it early enough in the morning, and *soba*, *udon* and *rāmen* can all be vegetarian if you ensure the soup stock is either vegetable or fish based, depending on your preferences. Traditional indigenous vegetarian cuisine, *shōjin*

home-made tofu restaurant

soba restaurant

ryōri, is served in many shotoku and in specialist restaurants, rather than sharing menu space with meat and fish dishes in any general-purpose restaurant. *Fucha ryōri*, which derives from the Chinese vegetarian tradition, is rarer still; Kyōto is a particularly good place to find it. Tourist Information Centres now carry lists of vegetarian and wholefood restaurants.

## Dining etiquette

Invitations to eat or drink are a serious business in Japan; try not to refuse, or offer an alternative date if you are not free when asked. Whoever extends the invitation pays; unless you're in a crowd of students or young people, sharing the cost (*warikan*) is uncommon, particularly where *gaijin* are involved.

### Courses

Japanese cuisine involves large numbers of relatively small dishes. There is no particular order in which they are consumed (though rice and *misoshiru* are generally

paired), nor need you finish one dish before proceeding to the next. Rice performs the function that bread or rolls do in a Western meal; rice bowls can be refilled as often as you like.

In a group-centred society like Japan, you need to join in the communal saying of 'passwords' before you can acceptably start drinking or eating.
They are:
■ **kanpai!** Figuratively = cheers!; literally = 'empty glass'
■ **itadakimasu!** Figuratively = tuck in!; literally = 'for what we are about to receive, we are truly grateful'
■ **gochisōsama (deshita)!** Figuratively = (it was a) great meal . . . thanks for your hospitality!; literally = 'what a feast'

sushi restaurant

# Phrasemaker

## Asking for a good eating place

| | |
|---|---|
| Is there a good restaurant near here? | **Kono chikaku ni ii resutoran wa arimasu ka?** |
| Are you open? | **Eigyō shite imasu ka?** |
| Do you take reservations/ bookings? | **Yoyaku wa dekimasu ka?** |
| I'd like to try the local speciality. | **Kono tochi no meibutsu ryōri o tabete mitain desu.** |

## Places to eat

| | |
|---|---|
| restaurant | **resutoran** |
| 'family' restaurant | **famirii resutoran** |
| fast food | **fasuto fūdo** |
| hamburger shop | **hanbāgā shoppu** |
| snack (light and quick meal) | **keishoku** |
| coffee seller/hot drinks stand | **kōhii sutando** |
| coffee shop | **kōhii shoppu** |
| canteen | **shokudō** |

## Adjectives

| | |
|---|---|
| expensive | **takai** |
| cheap/reasonable | **yasui** |
| high/first-class restaurant | **kōkyū resutoran** |
| ordinary | **futsūno** |
| well-known | **yūmeina** |
| delicious | **oishii** |
| quick | **hayai** |
| near | **chikai** |
| quiet | **shizukana** |
| good atmosphere | **fun'iki no ii** |
| good services | **sābisu no ii** |

## Arriving

| | |
|---|---|
| A table for (two/three), please. | **(Futari/Sannin) onegai shimasu.** |
| We have a reservation (for four). | **(Yonin) de yoyaku ga arimasu.** |
| Will you take us without a reservation? | **Yoyaku nashi de ii desu ka?** |
| Do you have any tables available? | **Seki wa arimasu ka?** |
| Non-smoking, please. | **Non-sumōkingu o onegai shimasu.** |

| | |
|---|---|
| **Go-yoyaku wa gozaimasu ka?** | Do you have a reservation? |
| **O-namae wa?** | Your name, please? |
| **Mōshiwake gozaimasen, tadaima manseki de gozaimasu.** | Sorry, we are full at the moment. |
| **O-machi itadake masu ka?** | Would you like to wait? |
| **O-matase itashimashita.** | Thank you for waiting. |
| **Dōzo, kochira e.** | This way, please. |

## Asking about the menu

| | |
|---|---|
| The menu, please. | **Menyū o (kudasai/onegai shimasu).** |
| Is there a ('special of the day'/ set menu)? | **('Honjitsu no tokubetsu menyū'/ Setto menyū) wa arimasu ka?** |
| What's today's (soup)? | **Kyō no (sūpu) wa nan desu ka?** |
| What do you recommend? | **O-susume wa nan desu ka?** |
| What's the local speciality? | **Kono tochi no meibutsu wa nan desu ka?** |
| What's that over there? | **Are wa nan desu ka?** |
| Have you got . . . ? | **. . . wa arimasu ka?** |
| What is . . . ? | **. . . toiu nowa nan desu ka?** |
| What is the chef's recommendation? | **Chefu no o-susume toiu nowa nan desu ka?** |

à la carte menu

sushi

## Items on the table

| | |
|---|---|
| chopsticks | **(o-)hashi** |
| fork | **fōku** |
| knife | **naifu** |
| napkin/serviette | **(tēburu) napukin** |
| spoon | **(o-)saji/supūn** |
| dish/plate | **(o-)sara** |
| saucer | **kōhii zara/sōsā** |
| salad bowl | **sarada bōru** |
| small/side plate | **kozara** |
| Japanese rice bowl | **(o-)chawan/gohan jawan** |
| Japanese lacquer soup bowl | **(o-)wan** |

## Ordering

| | |
|---|---|
| I'll have . . . | **(Watashi wa) . . . ni shimasu.** |
| I'll have the table d'hôte. | **Teishoku ni shimasu.** |
| I'll have this, please. | **Kore o onegai shimasu.** |
| I'll have . . . as the (starter). | **(Zensai/Sutātā) wa . . . ni shimasu.** |
| I'll have (fish/a steak) for the main course. | **Mein kōsu wa (o-sakana/ sutēki) ni shimasu.** |
| (Medium/Rare/Well-done), please. | **(Miidiamu/Rea/Uerudan) ni shite kudasai.** |
| No dessert, thank you. | **Dezāto wa irimasen.** |
| Yes, a (coffee/Japanese tea), please. | **Hai, (kōhii/Nihoncha) o onegai shimasu.** |
| May I have it right away, please. | **Sugu ni onegai shimasu.** |
| May I have everything together? | **Zenbu issho ni onegai shimasu.** |
| That's all, thank you. | **Sore de onegai shimasu.** |
| I will leave the choice to you. | **'Omakase' de onegai shimasu** |

| | |
|---|---|
| **Nani ni itashimashō ka?** | What would you like? |
| **O-kimari deshō ka?** | Are you ready to order? |
| **Honjitsu wa . . . de gozaimasu** | Today we have . . . |
| **Sutēki wa ikaga itashimashō ka?** | How would you like your steak done? |
| **Ato de (kōhii/dezāto) wa ikaga deshō ka?** | Would you like (coffee/dessert) later? |
| **O-nomimono wa?** | And to drink? |
| **Mōshiwake gozaimasen, . . . wa gozaimasen.** | Sorry, we don't have any . . . |
| **Shiromi no sakana de gozaimasu.** | It's a white fish. |
| **Kore wa kiku no isshu no yasai de gozaimasu.** | This vegetable is from the chrysanthemum family. |
| **Zeikomi de gozaimasu.** | Tax is included. |
| **Zeikin wa haitte orimasen.** | Tax is not included. |
| **Goyukkuri dōzo.** | Enjoy your meal. |

## Seasoning

| | |
|---|---|
| dressing | **doresshingu** |
| ketchup | **kechappu** |
| mayonnaise | **mayonēzu** |
| mustard | **karashi/masutādo** |
| Japanese green mustard | **wasabi** |
| oil | **oiru** |
| pepper | **koshō** |
| Japanese pepper (for noodles) | **shichimi (tōgarashi)** |
| salt | **(o-)shio** |
| soy sauce | **(o-)shōyu** |
| vinegar | **(o-)su** |
| Worcester-style thick sauce (for cutlets) | **sōsu** |

AFTER5 BEER STATION
屋上ビアガーデン
平日16:30-22:00 土・日・祝日15:00-20:30

## To drink

| | |
|---|---|
| One carafe of (well-warmed/slightly warmed) sake, please. | **(Atsukan/Nurukan) ippon kudasai.** |
| Could I have (plum wine/whisky with ice), please. | **(Umeshu/On za rokku) o onegai shimasu.** |
| one (full-sized) bottle/half-bottle (red/white/rose) wine | **(furu botoru/hāfu botoru) ippon (aka/shiro/rōze) wain** |
| beer | **biiru** |
| mineral water | **mineraru uōtā** |
| tap water | **(o-)mizu** |

miso soup

rice

## Eating habits

| | |
|---|---|
| I'm allergic to . . . | **(Watashi wa) . . . niwa arerugii o okoshimasu.** |
| I'm vegetarian. | **Bejitarian/Saishokushugi(sha) desu.** |
| Does it contain (shrimp/meat)? | **(Ebi/(O-)niku) wa haitte imasu ka?** |

## Politeness

| | |
|---|---|
| Let's start/Tuck in! | **Itadakimasu.** |
| Do you mind if I start before you? | **Osaki ni itadakimasu.** |
| Please start/don't wait for me. | **Osaki ni, dōzo.** |
| Cheers! | **Kanpai!** |

## During the meal

| | |
|---|---|
| Excuse me! | **Sumimasen!** |
| Waiter! | **Bōi-san!/Ueitā!** |
| What's this? | **Kore wa nan desu ka?** |
| How do we eat this? | **Kore wa dōyatte taberun desu ka?** |
| It's (cold/burnt). | **(Samete/Kogete) imasu.** |
| (This/My steak) is (undercooked/underdone). | **(Kore/Watashi no sutēki) wa (namanie/namayake) desu.** |
| This isn't what I ordered. | **Kore wa watashi ga chūmon shita mono dewa arimasen.** |
| My order hasn't come yet. | **Watashi no (o-)ryōri ga mada kite imasen.** |
| another bottle of . . . | **. . . o mō ippon** |
| A little more (water/bread/steamed rice), please. | **((O-)mizu/Pan/Raisu) o mōsukoshi kudasai.** |
| Where are the toilets? | **Toire wa doko desu ka?** |

| | |
|---|---|
| **Kono go-chūmon no o-kyaku-sama wa?** | Whose dish is this? |
| **Go-chūmon no shina wa ijō de yoroshii deshō ka?** | Have you had everything you ordered? |
| **Hoka ni nani ka (gozaimasu ka)?** | (Would you like) anything else? |

食券をお買い求め下さい。
中央の自動販売機で
お願いします。

Please ３ meal tickets

## Paying

| | |
|---|---|
| The bill, please. | **(O-kanjō/Shiharai) o onegai shimasu.** |
| Is tax included? | **Zeikomi desu ka?** |
| Do you take credit cards? | **Kurejitto kādo de haraemasu ka?** |
| There's a mistake, I think. | **Machigai ga aruyō desu.** |
| We didn't have any (beer/ice-cream). | **(Biiru/Aisu kuriimu) wa nomimasen/tabemasen deshita.** |
| Great meal/Thank you! | **Gochisōsama (deshita)!** |
| It was delicious! | **Oishikatta desu!** |

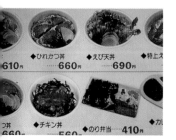

## Language works

open

### Arriving

**1** When you have a reservation

□ **Go-yoyaku wa gozaimasu ka?**

■ **Ramēru de yoyaku ga arimasu. Non-sumōkingu o onegai shimasu.**

□ **Dōzo, kochira e.**

What question did the waitress greet you with?

**2** When you don't have a reservation

□ **Seki wa arimasu ka? Futari desu.**

■ **Mōshiwake gozaimasen, tadaima manseki de gozaimasu. O-machi itadake masu ka? O-namae wa?**

Do you have someone with you?
Do you have to wait to be seated?

### Ordering

**3** Deciding what to have

□ **Nani ni itashimashō ka?**

■ **Mein kōsu wa sutēki ni shimasu.**

□ **Hai, kashikomari mashita. Sutēki wa ikaga itashimashō ka?**

■ **Rea ni shite kudasai.**

□ **Ato de kōhii wa ikaga deshō ka?**

■ **Iie, Nihoncha o onegai shimasu.**

What is your main course and how do you ask for it to be cooked?
What do you drink at the end of your meal?

**4** Having another drink

□ **O-nomimono wa?**

■ **Umeshu o onegai shimasu.**

□ **Mōshiwake gozaimasen. Umeshu wa gozaimasen ga.**

■ **A, sō desu ka. Jā . . . aka wain no furu botoru o ippon kudasai.**

What do you order first?
Why don't you get it?
Instead, you order a half bottle of white wine: true/false?

**5** When in doubt . . .

□ **Sumimasen! Kore wa dōyatte taberun desu ka?**

■ **Hai, sore wa . . .**

■ **Hoka ni nani ka gozaimasu ka?**

□ **Iie, arigatō.**

■ **Goyukkuri dōzo.**

What question do you ask the waitress?
What question does she ask you after she has solved your problem?

### The bill

**6** Paying

□ **O-kanjō o onegai shimasu. Kurejitto kādo de haraemasu ka?**

■ **Hai, kekkō de gozaimasu.**

□ **Gochisōsama deshita!**

■ **Oishikatta!**

How do you pay; in cash or by credit card?
Did you enjoy the meal?

prices

## Try it out

### Odd one out

Select the odd one out in each group.

a o-soba     udon
   rāmen      pan
b supagetti   tōsuto
   rōrupan    shokupan
c Asahi       Kirin
   Nihoncha   Sapporo

### At the table

What is the Japanese for the following?

1 chopsticks
2 fork
3 knife
4 napkin/serviette
5 spoon
6 salt
7 pepper

### As if you were there

Say the sentences below in Japanese. Use the words in brackets to help formulate them.

a Is there a good restaurant near here?
  ■ **(Kono chikaku ni . . .)**
b A table for two, please.
  ■ **(. . . onegai shimasu).**
c What's today's soup?
  ■ **(. . . nan desu ka?)**
d I'll have the tenpura, please.
  ■ **(Tenpura . . .)**
e One carafe of well-warmed sake, please.
  ■ **(. . . kudasai)**
f How do we eat this?
  ■ **(. . . taberun desu ka?)**
g It was delicious.
  ■ **(Oi . . .)**

tenpura

## Sound check

Some consonant sounds are altered, especially when they occur before particular vowels, such as **i**. For example:

**ci/si** is pronounced **shi** so 'similar' in Japanese becomes **shi-mi-rā**

**ti** is pronounced **chi**, so 'tip' in Japanese becomes **chippu**

If **t** occurs before the vowel **u**, it is pronounced **tsu** as in **tsunami** (tidal wave) so 'two' in Japanese is pronounced **tsū**.

breakfast

# Menu reader

## Types of food

**Furansupan** French bread
**Furenchi tōsuto** French toast
**gohan (rui/mono)** rice dishes
**men rui o-soba/udon/rāmen** Japanese noodle dishes
**niku ryōri** meat dishes

**pan** bread
**rōrupan** rolls
**sakana ryōri** fish dishes
**shōjin ryōri** vegetable dishes
**shokupan** sliced bread
**supagetti** Italian noodles
**tōsuto** toast

## Main ways of cooking

**abura de ageta/furai ni shita/tenpura ni shita** deep-fried
**itameta/furaipan de yaita** pan-fried
**karuku itameta/sotē ni shita** sautéed
**kunsei ni shita** smoked
**rōsuto shita/tenpi de yaita** roasted

**tenpi/ōbun de yaita** baked
**torobi de nikonda/shichū ni shita** stewed
**tsumemono ni shita** stuffed
**yaita** grilled
**yudeta** boiled

## The menu

**agemono** deep-fried foods (usually fish and vegetables)
**akadashi** red bean paste soup
**dezāto** dessert
**fugu** globefish
**furu kōsu** full meal (from the starter to dessert)
**furūtsu** fruit
**gobō** burdock (root vegetable common in Japan)
**gohan** steamed rice
**guriru** grill
**hamu** ham
**hasu** lotus (root vegetable grown in a pond)

**hireniku no guriru** grilled fillet (meat)
**honjitsu no niku ryōri** today's meat dish
**honjitsu no sūpu** soup of the day
**kaiseki ryōri** Japanese-style multi-course meal served at dinner parties/celebrations, with an emphasis on artistic presentation
**kisetsu no gohan** cooked rice with seasonal ingredients
**kisetsu no sakana ryōri** catch of the day
**kōsu** course

sushi

rāmen

nimono

**kobachi** small bowl (= small appetizer to enjoy while drinking sake)
**kōnomono** pickled vegetables such as radish, cucumber and aubergine
**mushimono** steamed foods (usually fish, shellfish and vegetables)
**namekowan** nameko mushroom broth
**niku ryōri** meat dish
**nimono** boiled and stewed foods, usually cooked in a broth of soy, **mirin** (sweet rice wine) and **dashi** (fish broth)
**ōdoburu** hors d'œuvre
**otsukuri** artistically presented assortment of sliced raw fish **(o-sashimi)**
**o-wan** soup bowl (= soup)
**potāju** soup/potage
**puroshūto hamu** Parma ham
**peti fūru** petit four
**sakana ryōri** fish dish(es)
**sāmon** salmon
**sarada** salad
**sashimi** sliced raw fish
**sashimi moriawase** assortment of sliced raw fish
**shābetto** sorbet
**shabu-shabu** paper-thin sliced beef (self-) cooked at the table in broth
**shiizā sarada** Caesar salad
**shiitake** large wild mushroom
**shūkuriimu** cream puff
**soba** buckwheat

noodles
**soba kaiseki** multi-course meal, with buckwheat noodes as the entrée
**suimono** clear soup
**sukiyaki** cook-yourself pot dish with meat and vegetables
**sumōku sāmon (Noruuē san)** smoked salmon (produced in Norway)
**sunomono** small Japanese-style salad using vegetables or seafood dressed with vinegar and seasoning
**supagetti** spaghetti
**sushi** vinegared rice containing raw or grilled fish, eggs and vegetables formed into a variety of shapes, eg balls, ovals, rolls
**sushi moriawase** assortment of sushi pieces
**sushi kaiseki** multi-course meal, with artistically-presented sushi assortment as the entrée
**tenpura** vegetables and fish battered in wheat flour and egg, deep-fried in vegetable oil
**tsukemono** vegetables pickled in rice bran and/or salt
**tsukidashi** small appetizer served with sake
**udon** thick, white noodles made from wheat flour
**yakimono** grilled foods
**yasai** vegetable(s)
**yasai moriawase** mixed vegetables/salad

miso soup

gohan

tenpura

# The drinks

## Specialities

| | |
|---|---|
| well-warmed sake | **atsukan** |
| slightly warmed sake | **nurukan** |
| unheated sake | **reishu/hiyazake** |
| brandy | **burandē, Kamyu, Naporeon** |
| champagne | **shanpen** |
| whisky | **uisukii, Barantain, Ōrudopā, Shiibasu Riigaru** |
| whisky and water | **mizuwari** |
| whisky over ice | **on za rokku** |

## Wines

| | |
|---|---|
| dry | **karakuchi** |
| sweet | **amakuchi** |
| bottle | **furu botoru** |
| half-bottle | **hāfu botoru** |
| glass | **gurasu** |
| imported wine | **yunyū wain** |
| French wine | **Furansu(san) wain** |
| German wine | **Doitsu(san) wain** |
| domestic wine | **kokusan wain** |
| apple wine | **ringo wain** |
| apricot wine | **anzu wain** |

## Hot drinks

| | |
|---|---|
| Japanese green tea | **o-cha/Nihoncha** |
| tea | **kōcha** |
| coffee | **kōhii** |

## Street eating

**amaguri** roasted chestnuts
**ikayaki** grilled squid
**okonomiyaki** a cross between a Spanish omelette and a savoury pancake
**ōbanyaki** muffin-like tea cakes containing sautéed sweetened azuki beans
**takoyaki** golf-ball-sized savoury nuggets of fried vegetable, flour and octopus
**yakisoba** pan-fried noodles with cabbage and meat
**yakitōmorokoshi** grilled corn-on-the-cob basted with soy sauce
**wataame** candy floss

# Entertainment and leisure

kabuki actor

## Cultural life

Japan's cultural life is rich and varied: fine arts and handicrafts, design, fashion and performing arts all enjoy high social status and command followings more often associated in the West with popstars.

Among the most interesting experiences can be found in the colour and ambience of Japan's traditional performing arts. The buildings which house several of these arguably justify a visit in their own right. The *Kokuritsu Gekijō* is Japan's National Theatre (Nagatachō, Tōkyō); the *Kabuki-za* (Ginza, Tōkyō) is the national centre for *kabuki*, Japan's colourful all-male traditional theatre.

Japan's wealth and reputation for cultural appreciation ensures that the world's great performing companies always include Tōkyō in their itineraries. Whether performed by the Tōkyō Symphony Orchestra or the Berlin Philharmonic, a classical concert in Suntory Hall (Akasaka) is an experience worth having. The same is true of modern music, which has spawned countless imitators in Japan; Tōkyō's Yoyogi-kōen Park on Sunday afternoons provides a showcase of different styles. There are a few notable exceptions to the trend for imitation over originality: Watanabe Sadao for jazz aficionados, Orquesta de la Luz for devotees of *salsa*.

### Cultural events for visitors

Traditional performing arts include *Noh* and *kabuki* theatre, *kyōgen* (short traditional comedy in colloquial Japanese), *bunraku* (traditional puppet theatre) and *Gagaku* (classical court music played by a 16-member orchestra). *Noh*, the older high-theatre of masks, is longer and difficult to follow; *kabuki* is more colourful and penetrable. Despite both being entirely in Japanese, it is possible to get English-language programmes in some Tōkyō and Kyōto theatres. Before buying a ticket, try watching a period drama on television to see if you like it; if still undecided, you can buy tickets for a single act.

The Tea Ceremony (*cha-no-yu*) offers a uniquely Japanese experience, affording insights into Japanese etiquette, cuisine and even interior design. Hotels in Tōkyō and Ōsaka stage shortened versions daily; Kyōto is the best place for the real thing, teahouse included. Contact the Urasenke Foundation, Japan's largest tea 'school' for details. *Kaiseki* is the banquet served after *cha-no-yu*, worth trying at least once.

Ikebana International runs short courses for foreigners in the Japanese art of flower arrangement.

theatre entrance

**Pachinko**

*Pachinko* is a version of pinball which the Japanese have adapted to their built-up environment. It is played, usually by adults, seated at vertical machines (this means that many machines can be crowded into a small *pachinko-ya* (parlour)).

Most players generally express little outward emotion, although the noise of the pinballs can be deafening. There tends to be a rather sleazy aura surrounding many of the parlours, reflecting their links with the *yakuza*, Japan's underworld.

## Outdoor activities

Mountains cover as much as 80% of Japan's terrain. Hill walking and climbing are pleasant, relaxing and visually stimulating; they're also cheap, even if the alpine accommodation isn't always. At weekends, rural Japanese families enjoy taking to the hills to collect wild mushrooms which make a delicious accompaniment to a Japanese meal.

### Active sports

Visitors encounter the same problems here as the Japanese: lack of space, crowds and high costs.

**Golf** is extremely popular throughout Japan, but public courses are over-crowded, and getting to and from them means a very early rise, not to mention substantial fees; **tennis** poses similar problems.

More cost-effective and time-efficient are multi-storey driving ranges, where you can sometimes also hit baseballs. While **beaches** and **pools** are not expensive, travel time and crowding make them unappealing. **Water sports** are best on caldera lakes (lakes in the craters of extinct volcanoes) in Kyūshū; the best **surfing** and **diving** is in Okinawa, but it's a long way south.

**Snow skiing** in Honshū is accessible, if you can cope with the crowds and smallish slopes; if you're prepared to travel further afield to Hokkaidō, the resorts are bigger and better (Furano and Niseko), and downhill skiing is augmented by cross country. The 1972 Winter Olympics were staged in Sapporo (capital of Hokkaidō), and Nagano, 90 minutes north-west of Tōkyō by train, was the site of the 1998 Winter Games. Both are worth a visit; the facilities are first rate.

Where is a good place to go for skiing?

**Sukii niwa doko ga ii desu ka?**

## Passive sports

Spectator sports are more accessible and affordable, particularly if your visit is short.

**Baseball** is hugely popular and well-played by a thriving professional league (the Yomiuri Giants playing in the Tōkyō Dōmu would be a match worth seeing). The more popular – and therefore more expensive – games are played in the evenings by floodlight.

Japan's economic status makes it a key stop on the travelling global circuits of high-profile sports, like ATP **tennis** tour. It hosts several prestigious golf tournaments each year, as well as the final **Formula I Grand Prix** race of the season, at Suzuka, each October.

Along with Korea, Japan will jointly stage the soccer World Cup in 2002. The J-League, Japan's first professional **soccer** league, may eventually do for soccer what has been achieved in baseball. For the present, a J-League match is more of a window on what 2002 will be like than an opportunity to view top-class sport.

## Traditional martial arts

**Sumō** is a highly stylised form of wrestling indigenous to Japan which has become a popular national sport, commonly associated with the heavyweight division. Sumō tournaments (in Tōkyō, staged at the *Ryōgoku Kokugikan*) provide real insights into the Japanese character: see if you can figure out why there are so many single women in the audiences! You can also visit training 'stables' to see stars of the future in the making and, to round your day off nicely, have a *chanko nabe* meal (stockpot stew cooked in cast iron pots and served to sumō wrestlers in training) in one of the numerous restaurants run by retired

wrestlers. Other martial arts include:

**aikidō** art of self-defence in which the attacker's own momentum is turned against him

**jūdō** self-defence sport originating in the Edo period (1600–1637), using hands and arms instead of weapons and based on the principle of utilising an opponent's own strength and weight to destabilise his balance

**karate** combat art in which hands, elbow, knees and feet are all used as weapons of defence against an attacker

**kendō** Japanese fencing

**kyūdō** Japanese archery

❗ Where can I buy tickets for the sumō tournament at the Kokugikan?
**Kokugikan deno sumō no nyūjōken wa doko de kaemasu ka?**

# Phrasemaker

## Getting to know the place

| | |
|---|---|
| Do you have (a town plan/ an entertainment guide)? | **(Taun mappu/Jōhōshi) wa arimasu ka?** |
| Do you have any information in (English)? | **(Eigo) deno jōhō wa arimasu ka?** |
| I'd like to join a city tour. | **Shinai kankō o shitain desu ga.** |
| Is there a guided (tour/bus tour)? | **Gaido tsuki (no kankō annai/ basu tsuā) wa arimasu ka?** |
| Are there any (cinemas/ theatres)? | **(Eigakan/Gekijō) wa arimasu ka?** |
| Could you recommend a restaurant? | **Resutoran o suisen shite kudasai?** |
| Where is a good place to go for (sightseeing/skiing)? | **(Kankō/Sukii) niwa doko ga ii desu ka?** |
| Is there anything for children? | **Kodomo tachi ga tanoshimeru tokoro wa arimasu ka?** |
| | |
| **(Eigo o hanasu) gaido/tenjōin** | (English-speaking) tour guide/ bus tour attendant |
| **(hannichi/ichinichi) kōsu** | (half-day/one-day) tour |
| **shokuji tsuki** | dinner included |
| **tsūyaku** | interpreter |

leaflets

| | | |
|---|---|---|
| **Gaido tsuki no tsuā ga arimasu.** | | There's a guided tour. |
| **Panfuretto o dōzo.** | | Here is a brochure. |
| **Donna koto ga shitai desu ka?** | | What are you interested in? |
| **(Bunraku/Kyōgen) ga omoshiroi kamo shiremasen.** | | You may be interested in (traditional puppet theatre/comedy). |
| **(Kyōto/Nagano) wa dō desu ka?** | | How about a visit to (Kyōto/Nagano)? |
| **Tōkyō kara sukii gerende made tatta (san) jikan desu.** | | It takes only (three) hours to get to a ski resort from Tokyo. |
| **Urayasu ni arimasu.** | | It's in Urayasu. |

rock garden at Ryōanji Temple, Kyōto

| | |
|---|---|
| art gallery | **bijutsukan/garō** |
| ballet | **barē** |
| castle | **(o-)shiro** |
| cinema | **eigakan** |
| concert | **konsāto** |
| discotheque | **disūko** |
| exhibition | **tenrankai** |
| festival | **(o-)matsuri** |
| fireworks display | **hanabi taikai** |
| lake | **mizuumi** |
| museum | **hakubutsukan** |
| musical | **myūjikaru** |
| opera | **opera** |
| park | **kōen** |
| snow festival | **yuki matsuri** |
| theatre | **gekijō** |
| theme park | **tēma pāku** |
| vaudeville/variety theatre | **engeijō** |
| zoo | **dōbutsuen** |
| (traditional) comic storytelling | **rakugo** |
| emperor's palace | **kōkyo** |
| (Japanese) garden | **(Nihon) teien** |
| karaoke bar | **karaoke** |
| pinball parlour | **pachinko-ya** |
| shrine | **jinja** |
| storytellers' hall | **yose** |
| temple | **(o-)tera** |
| waterfall | **taki** |

Imperial Theatre

帝
国
劇
場

## Getting more information

| | |
|---|---|
| Where is (the swimming pool/ the concert hall)? | **(Pūru/Konsāto hōru) wa doko ni arimasu ka?** |
| Where does the (coach tour) start from? | **(Basu tsuā) wa doko kara demasu ka?** |
| What time does it (start/finish)? | **Nanji ni (sutāto shimasu/owari masu) ka?** |
| When does it open? | **Itsu akimasu ka?** |
| Do we need tickets? | **(Chiketto/Nyūjōken*) wa hitsuyō desu ka?** |
| Are there any tickets? | **(Chiketto/Nyūjōken) wa arimasu ka?** |
| How much is it? | **Ikura desu ka?** |
| Where can we buy tickets? | **Doko de (chiketto/nyūjōken) o kaemasu ka?** |

**Chiketto** is a more modern word for 'ticket', used for transport and other 'recent' inventions.
**Nyūjōken** is a more traditional word meaning 'to enter a place'. If in doubt use **chiketto**.

拝観料　大人(Adult) 500円(yen)
Admission Fee 小人(Child) 200円(yen)
団体割引(30人以上) a discount for parties (more 30 persons)

開館時間　Display hours are
3月～10月
(Mar～Oct)　9：00A.M～4：30P.M
11月～2月
(Nov～Feb)　9：00A.M～4：00P.M

毎月第三金曜日休館
Closed on third friday every month

長野市観光情報センター
Nagano City Tourist Information Center

## Getting in

| | |
|---|---|
| **(Chiketto/Nyūjōken) o katte kudasai.** | You must buy a ticket. |
| **(Chiketto/Nyūjōken) wa hitsuyō arimasen.** | You don't need a ticket. |
| **Nyūjō muryō desu.** | There's no entrance fee. |
| (Two) tickets for (Saturday/ today/tomorrow), please. | **(Doyōbi/Kyō/Ashita) no chiketto o (ni) mai kudasai.** |
| Is there a programme? | **Puroguramu wa arimasu ka?** |
| Is there an (interval/ intermission)? | **(Intābaru/Kyūkei) wa arimasu ka?** |
| Are the seats numbered? | **Seki niwa bangō ga tsuite imasu ka?** |
| Is this seat available? | **Kono seki wa aite imasu ka?** |
| What is there to do in Okinawa? | **Okinawa dewa donna koto ga dekimasu ka?** |
| How do we get to Mount Fuji from here? | **Koko kara Fuji-san made wa dōyatte ikimasu ka?** |

| | |
|---|---|
| **Hai, kodomo wa hangaku desu.** | Yes, it's half price for children. |
| **(Honjitsu/Tōjitsu) nomi yūkō desu.** | It's valid for (today only/the date specified). |
| **(Nijuppun) no kyūkei ga ikkai arimasu.** | There is one interval of (20 minutes). |
| **Achira no baiten ni arimasu.** | They are sold at the shop over there. |
| **(Aite imasu/Aite imasen.)** | It's (available/taken). |
| **Sumimasen, urikire desu.** | Sorry, it's sold out. |
| **Chizu dewa koko ni arimasu.** | It's here on the map. |
| **Tōkyō eki kara** | from Tokyo station |
| **(chiketto/nyūjōken) uriba desu** | at the ticket office |
| **Gozen (kuji han) kara yoru no (hachiji) made** | from (9.30) am to (8)pm |

## In a theatre

| | |
|---|---|
| bar | **bā** |
| cloakroom | **kurōku/tenimotsu azukarijo** |
| entrance | **iriguchi** |
| exit | **deguchi** |
| information desk | **annaijo** |
| row | **retsu** |
| seat | **seki/zaseki** |
| shop | **baiten** |
| stairs/staircase | **kaidan** |
| powder room/toilets | **keshōshitsu/toire** |
| Gents | **tonogata** |
| Ladies | **gofujin** |

## Charges and cancellations

| | |
|---|---|
| surcharge | **tsuika ryōkin** |
| admission fee (general) | **nyūjōryo** |
| (for shrines and temples) | **(haikanryō)** |
| free admission | **nyūjō muryō** |
| cancellation | **kyanseru/torikeshi** |
| charged | **yūryō** |
| postponement | **enki** |
| reservation | **yoyaku** |
| sold out | **urikire** |
| ticket | **chiketto/ken/nyūjōken** |

theatre entrance

## Sports and outdoor activities

Where can I (play squash/go swimming)?
**Doko de (sukasshu/oyogukoto) ga dekimasu ka?**

Can we play (golf/tennis) here?
**Koko dewa (gorufu/tenisu) wa dekimasu ka?**

Can we use the hotel swimming pool?
**Hoteru no pūru wa tsukae masu ka?**

Where are the (changing rooms/showers)?
**(Kōishitsu/Shawā) wa doko desu ka?**

I'd like to hire (a surfboard/balls).
**(Sāfubōdo/Bōru) o karitain desu ga.**

One racket and two balls, please.
**Raketto ippon to bōru niko onegai shimasu.**

I'd like to take (skiing/snowboarding) lessons.
**(Sukii/Sunōbōdo) no ressun o uketain desu ga.**

We would like to ski in Hokkaido.
**Hokkaidō de sukii o shitain desu ga.**

I'd like to see a night baseball game at the Tōkyō Dome.
**'Tōkyō Dōmu' de naitā o mitain desu ga.**

I'd like to (dive/go windsurfing) in Okinawa.
**Okinawa de (daibingu/sāfin) o shitain desu ga.**

Where can I buy tickets for the sumō tournament at the Kokugikan?
**Kokugikan deno sumō no nyūjōken wa doko de kaemasu ka?**

Can we hire a full set of ski equipment?
**Sukii no dōgu o isshiki karirukoto wa dekimasu ka?**

**Sukii sukūru de mōshi konde kudasai.**
Please apply for it at the ski school.

**Kore ga mōshikomisho desu.**
Here is an application form.

**Iriguchi de tōjitsuken o katte kudasai.**
Please purchase a day-ticket(s) at the entrance.

**Panfuretto ga arimasu.**
We have brochures.

**Purei gaido ni toiawasete kudasai.**
Please enquire at the Play Guide agency.

No entry to the woods

## On land

| | |
|---|---|
| baseball | **yakyū** |
| night game/ 'nighter' | **naitā** |
| climbing | **tozan/yama nobori** |
| cycling | **saikuringu** |
| golf | **gorufu** |
| horse racing | **keiba** |
| soccer | **sakkā** |
| ten-pin bowling | **bōringu** |
| tennis | **tenisu** |
| volleyball | **barēbōru** |

## On the slopes and in the water

| | |
|---|---|
| diving | **daibingu** |
| fishing | **tsuri** |
| skiing | **sukii** |
| snowboarding | **sunōbōdo** |
| surfing | **sāfin** |
| swimming | **suiei** |
| swimming in the sea | **kaisuiyoku** |
| water-skiing | **suijō sukii** |

## Sporting places

| | |
|---|---|
| baseball ground | **yakyūjō** |
| beach | **kaigan** |
| golf course | **gorufujō** |
| golf range | **gorufu renshūjō** |
| racecourse | **keibajō** |
| ski slope/resort | **sukiijō** |
| soccer field/ pitch | **sakkājō** |
| swimming pool | **pūru** |
| ten-pin bowling alley | **bōringujō** |
| tennis court | **tenisu kōto** |

## Equipment

| | |
|---|---|
| ball | **bōru** |
| (rented) bicycle | **(kashi) jitensha** |
| golf club | **gorufu no kurabu** |
| surfboard | **sāfubōdo** |
| ski | **sukii ita** |
| ski boots | **sukii gutsu** |
| snowboard | **sunōbōdo** |
| bathing suit | **mizugi (women) kaisui pantsu (men)** |
| racket | **raketto** |

## Language works

## Getting to know the place

**1** Going on a city tour
- ☐ **Shinai kankō o shitain desu ga.**
- ■ **Hai.**
- ☐ **Gaido tsuki no basu tsuā wa arimasu ka?**
- ■ **Hai. Ichinichi kōsu to hannichi kōsu ga arimasu. Panfuretto o dōzo.**

What length of tour can you choose from?
What are you given?

## Getting more information

**2** Enjoy the concert!
- ☐ **Konsāto hōru wa doko ni arimasu ka?**
- ■ **Tōkyō eki kara . . .**
  . . .
- ☐ **Doko de chiketto o kaemasu ka?**
- ■ **Chiketto wa hitsuyō arimasen. Nyūjō muryō desu.**

Do you have to pay for a ticket?

## Getting in

**3** Buying tickets
- ☐ **Kyō no chiketto o 2 (ni) mai kudasai.**
- ■ **Hai, dōzo.**
- ☐ **Puroguramu wa arimasu ka?**
- ■ **Achira no baiten ni arimasu.**
- ☐ **Seki niwa bangō ga tsuite imasu ka?**
- ■ **Hai, tsuite imasu.**
- ☐ **Intābaru wa arimasu ka?**
- ■ **Nijuppun pun no kyūkei ga ikkai arimasu.**

What do you ask for after you have got your tickets?
Is there an interval?

## Sports and outdoor activities

**4** At a travel agency
- ☐ **Donna supōtsu ga ii desu ka?**
- ■ **'Tōkyō Dōmu' de naitā o mitain desu ga.**
- ☐ **Urikire desu. Iriguchi de tōjitsuken o katte kudasai.**
- ■ **Kokugikan deno sumō no nyūjōken wa doko de kaemasu ka?**
- ☐ **Purei gaido ni toiawasete kudasai.**

What two sports are you interested in watching?
Did you manage to get any tickets at all from this travel agent?

本日の開閉時間

| | | |
|---|---|---|
| 開門 午前 | 5時00分 |
| 閉門 午後 | 6時20分 |

opening and closing times

## Try it out

### Name it

Find the correct Japanese terms for these.

1 Japanese castle
2 Japanese garden
3 park
4 shrine
5 temple

| | |
|---|---|
| taki | o-tera |
| o-shiro | o-matsuri |
| mizuumi | kōen |
| jinja | kōkyo |
| karaoke | Nihon teien |

### Mix and match

Match the first half of each sentence (1–5) with its second half (a–e).

1 Taun mappu
2 Donna koto
3 Ikura
4 Doko de oyogukoto
5 Sukii no dōgu

a ga shitai desu ka?
b ga dekimasu ka?
c o isshiki karirukoto ga dekimasu ka?
d wa arimasu ka?
e desu ka?

## As if you were there

Give the Japanese for the phrases in brackets.

a ☐ (Are there any tickets?)
  ■ **Sumimasen, urikire desu.**
b ☐ (Is this seat available?)
  ■ **Aite imasu.**
c ☐ **Donna supōtsu ga ii desu ka?**
  ■ (We would like to ski in Hokkaidō.)

## Sound check

The only consonant which is pronounced on its own is **n**, which is sometimes spoken nasally and is like the **ng** at the end of **sing** and sometimes like **m** or **n**. Also, **th** is pronounced **s** and combined with an appropriate vowel sound.
Think becomes **shink**
Thatcher becomes **Satchā**
When doing business, until you know your Japanese counterparts well, you might consider pronouncing your own name and possibly your company's name as the Japanese would. If your **meishi** (business card) has been translated into Japanese, you can do this merely by reading the *katakana* according to the Japanese sound system.

# Emergencies

## Tourist information

When it comes to providing information for visitors, Japan is highly organised. The Japan National Tourist Organisation (JNTO) has numerous overseas offices, including in Australia,

fire hydrant

Britain, Canada and the USA. It operates Tourist Information Centres (TICs) at Narita Airport ((0476) 34-6251), in central Tōkyō ((03) 3201-3331) and Kyōto ((075) 371-5649) for overseas visitors. English-language tourist information is available by telephone through JNTO's *Japan Travel-Phone* (0088) 22-2800 for Eastern Japan, (0088) 22-4800 for Western Japan (the call is free outside Tōkyō); 3503-4400 in Tōkyō) and from DialService's *Japan Hotline* ((03) 3586-0110).

Major tourist sights throughout Japan also have *annaijo* (information offices) which are more geared to providing tourist literature and Japanese-language information. The Japan Travel Bureau (JTB) is a semi-governmental travel agency with numerous offices throughout Japan and overseas. It publishes a range of guides as well as arranging travel and sightseeing. Guides may be arranged directly through the Japan Guide Association ((03) 3213-2706); JNTO also operates a volunteer programme, *Goodwill Guides*.

## Personal safety

Japan is rightly famous for offering visitors very high levels of personal security, despite having one of the world's largest criminal fraternities,

the *yakuza*; they confine their activities strictly to other Japanese. Although it is possible to have your pocket picked at Narita or Kansai Airport, you are far more likely to suffer a loss by forgetting personal belongings. Returning to where you think you lost something, or a phone call to a Lost and Found Office in Japan frequently results in success. Useful phone numbers are:
Tōkyō Underground (TRTA)
(03) 3834-5577
JR East (trains)
(03) 3423-0111
Toei Underground and Buses
(03) 5600-2029
Tōkyō Taxis
(03) 3648-0300

**❗** Please call the police for me.
**Keisatsu o yonde kudasai.**

## Earthquakes

The Kōbe earthquake (1995) and the anticipation of a widely predicted quake in the Kantō (Tōkyō) region mean that visitors should be prudent rather than paranoid. Locate the emergency exits and nearest fire extinguisher wherever you are staying, as well as your designated assembly point. You may feel reassured by leaving your shoes beside your door, since broken glass is a major quake hazard; good hotels will include an emergency action plan in the room,

fire engine

and it's wise to familiarize yourself with it. The Japanese measure quakes in

立入禁止
KEEP OUT

terms of *shindo*, which is roughly the equivalent of the Richter Scale.

**Shindo ratings**
**Shindo 1 (ichi)** only some feel the quake
**Shindo 2 (ni)** a majority of people can feel the quake; wall-hangings tremble slightly
**Shindo 3 (san)** houses tremble; wall-hangings vigorously
**Shindo 4 (yon)** houses are rocked vigorously; anyone on the street can feel the quake
**Shindo 5 (go)** books fall from shelves; some people are unable to walk
**Shindo 6 (roku)** most people cannot stand up; landslides and fissures occur
**Shindo 7 (nana)** fault lines begin to appear on the landscape.

The Great Hanshin Quake (Kōbe) in 1995 was Shindo 7.2.

## Nuisances

'No Smoking' signs are widely ignored in Japan; no-smoking seats and facilities throughout Japan are more limited, so book early if you are particularly bothered by smokers.

Female visitors need to be aware of groping hands when travelling on crowded commuter trains. Unsolicited comments on the street or a station platform from *sarariimen* returning home late in the evening having had a few drinks are, at worst, a harmless nuisance.

You will find it helpful to carry a supply of paper tissues everywhere, especially in summer. Fabric handkerchiefs are only used for wiping your brow or drying your hands; use only paper tissues for blowing your nose – the Japanese consider it unhygienic to use anything else – and be discrete:

sneezing and coughing in public is not as acceptable as it is in the West. Japanese-style squat toilets (*benjo*), more common in towns and rural areas, often do not have toilet paper, giving added value to your paper tissues. Don't be shocked if you encounter mixed-sex toilets; department stores and office buildings offer much better facilities – even electric seat warmers and 'showerlets' (warm water jet in place of toilet paper) on occasion.

In drinking quarters, Japanese men blithely urinate against buildings and walls; spitting, unfortunately, is also tolerated.

## Staying healthy

It is advisable to take out maximum medical cover. If you are already being treated, it may be advisable to carry a letter from your doctor explaining your condition and treatment, as well as carrying a supply of your prescribed medication.

The strength of Japanese over-the-counter pharmaceuticals is less than their Western equivalents, so it is advisable to take a supply of aspirin/paracetamol and, if you need them, antihistamine tablets. In summer, calamine lotion provides relief from insect bites. Sun block and sun-tan lotion can be expensive, so you should take an adequate supply with you. It is also advisable to bring your own contraceptive pills (and to pack these discretely, as they are illegal in Japan and may be confiscated).

The food and water are universally safe to consume; if your stomach doesn't travel well, however, bring a kaolin preparation. The epidemic of food poisoning in Sakai in 1996 was the exception which proves the rule;

take care if you pick wild mushrooms.

English-speaking doctors and dentists, clinics and Western-style pharmacies exist but are in a distinct minority; medical services are expensive. Japan operates a specialist rather than a general practitioner system; medical practitioners and clinics are generally private (although big, urban hospitals are publicly run).

Prescribed drugs are most commonly sold by the prescribing doctor or clinic. Western pharmaceuticals are available in Tōkyō at the American Pharmacy ((03) 3436-3028) in Hibiya, only a stone's throw away from the Tōkyō TIC.

If you need a doctor, try contacting the Tōkyō TIC for advice, since it keeps a list of English-speaking doctors; consult your Embassy for doctors who speak your mother tongue. English-speaking medical services are also available from:

**Hospital Information**
(03) 3213-2323
**Japan Helpline (24hrs)**
(0120) 461-997
**Tōkyō Medical and Surgical Clinic**
(03) 3436-3028
**International Clinic**
(03) 3583-7831

Is there someone here who speaks English?
**Eigo o hanaseru hito wa imasu ka?**

## Telephones

Public telephones abound, in colour as well as quantity. Pink and red telephones take ¥10 coins only, the cost of a three-minute local call; yellow and blue telephones take ¥100 coins as well. Green telephones take coins, pre-paid cards and credit cards; some have two receivers. Telephone cards are widely available, including from vending machines; visitors usually find ¥500 or ¥1,000 phone cards easier to use than coins.

International calls must be made from grey telephones. International telephone services have been deregulated in Japan, with the result that you can choose which company you route your call through. The three main providers are KDD, ITJ and IDC.

**Directory Enquiries** 104
**domestic area codes**
| | |
|---|---|
| Tōkyō | 03 |
| Narita | 0476 |
| Ōsaka | 06 |
| Kyōto | 075 |
| Nagoya | 052 |
| Sapporo | 011 |

**English-language Directory Enquiries**
(03) 5295-1010 (Tōkyō)
(06) 313-1010 (Ōsaka)
**international access numbers**
001 (KDD)
0041 (ITJ)
0061 (IDC)
**your home country direct**
0039 + country code + 1
**International Operator** 0051
**Emergency telephone numbers**
(Japanese-language services are shown in bold)
| | |
|---|---|
| Police | **110** |
| Ambulance/Fire | **119** |

(03) 3212-2323 (offers English-language advice on the nearest available medical treatment)
**Tōkyō English Lifeline (TELL)**
(03) 5721-4347

## Postal facilities and services

Postal services in Japan are safe and efficient; post can be sent to and from Japan using *rōmaji* (Roman letters), provided the lettering is clear (use BLOCK CAPITALS). The postal service logo is **〒** in red and white. Post boxes are usually red for normal delivery, blue for special delivery.

Rates range from ¥70 for international postcards (*hagaki*) to ¥100–120 for airmail letters (*shojō*) of up to 10 grams to North America, Australasia and Western Europe.

Main post offices are open weekdays until 7 pm, Saturdays until 5 pm and Sunday mornings until 12.30 pm; local post offices close at 5 pm on weekdays, 3 pm on Saturdays. Main post offices offer foreign exchange, traveller's cheque and fax services; they also sell cardboard boxes for mailing things abroad.

## Newspapers, radio and television

Japan has become the supreme *jōhō shakai* (information society). The sheer volume of information, however, can be overwhelming; enormous variations in quality place a premium on being discriminating.

Japan's quality national press publish morning and evening Japanese editions, as well as English-language editions, the only non-Japanese language papers widely available. The *Japan Times* (morning) is the most widely read by visitors, often for its Classified Pages; the *Daily Yomiuri* (morning) runs articles from British and American papers. The *Asahi Evening News* is the only afternoon edition. All are widely available at major hotels, bookshops and station kiosks.

The *Nikkei Weekly* is Japan's leading English-language business paper, and both the *Financial Times* and *(Asian) Wall Street Journal* publish English-language editions in Japan.

Television is a better source of information than radio, where the choice is largely limited to FEN (American armed forces' Far East Network, on AM) and J-Wave (FM). NHK, Japan's public service provider, broadcasts bilingual evening news reports. Up-market hotels offer CNN, Sky and BBC World satellite services, and many hotels offer (pay) cable television (JCTV) with adapters enabling English-language programmes to be received in English.

## Embassy addresses

**Australia** 2-1-14, Mita, Minato-ku, Tōkyō 108
(03) 5232-4111
**Canada** 7-3-38, Akasaka, Minato-ku, Tōkyō 107
(03) 3408-2101/8
**Eire** Kowa #25 Building, 8-7, Sanbanchō, Chiyoda-ku, Tōkyō 102
(03) 3263-0695
**New Zealand** 20-40, Kamiyamachō, Shibuya-ku, Tōkyō 150
(03) 3467-2271
**South Africa** 414 Zenkyoran Building, 2-7-9, Hirakawa-chō, Chiyoda-ku, Tōkyō 102
(03) 3265-3366
**United Kingdom** 1, Ichibanchō, Chiyoda-ku, Tōkyō 102
(03) 3265-5511
**United States of America** 1-10-5, Akasaka, Minato-ku, Tōkyō 107
(03) 3224-5000

# Phrasemaker

## General

| | |
|---|---|
| Help! | **Tasukete!** |
| Excuse me/Hello! (to attract attention) | **Sumimasen!** |
| Can you help me? | **Tasukete kudasai.** |
| Where is the (police station/ police box/hospital)? | **(Keisatsu/Kōban/Byōin) wa doko desu ka?** |
| Go away/Leave me alone! | **Doite kudasai!** |
| I'll call the police. | **Keikan o yobimasu.** |
| Please call the (police/ fire engine) for me. | **(Keisatsu/Shōbōsha) o yonde kudasai.** |
| Please telephone this number for me. | **Koko ni denwa o kakete kudasai.** |

## Health

| | |
|---|---|
| Call me (a doctor/an ambulance). | **(O-isha-san/Kyūkyūsha) o yonde kudasai.** |
| It's urgent. | **Kinkyū desu.** |
| Is there someone here who speaks English? | **Eigo o hanaseru hito wa imasu ka?** |

| | |
|---|---|
| **Dō shitan desu ka?** | What's the matter with you? |
| **Wakarimashita.** | I understand. |
| **Matte ite kudasai.** | Please wait. |
| **Sugu yonde kimasu.** | I'll go and call immediately. |
| **Issho ni kite kudasai.** | Please come with me. |
| **Dareka ni renraku o shimasu ka?** | Would you like me to contact anyone for you? |

## Parts of the body

| | | | |
|---|---|---|---|
| body | **karada** | chest | **mune** |
| head | **atama** | abdomen | **fukubu/onaka** |
| face | **kao** | stomach | **i** |
| eye(s) | **me** | liver | **kanzō** |
| hair | **kami/** | kidney | **jinzō** |
| | **kaminoke** | intestine | **chō** |
| nose | **hana** | pancreas | **suizō** |
| mouth | **kuchi** | arm(s) | **ude** |
| tongue | **shita/bero** | hand(s) | **te** |
| chin/jaw | **ago** | elbow(s) | **hiji** |
| ear/s | **mimi** | finger(s) | **yubi** |
| external ear | **gaiji** | thumb(s) | **oyayubi** |
| middle ear | **chūji** | nail(s) | **tsume** |
| inner ear | **naiji** | hip(s) | **koshi** |
| tooth/teeth | **ha** | buttock(s) | **(o-)shiri** |
| throat | **nodo** | thigh(s) | **momo** |
| oesophagus/ | **shokudō** | leg(s) | **ashi** |
| gullet | | foot/feet | **ashi** |
| neck | **kubi** | knee(s) | **hiza** |
| back | **senaka** | toe(s) | **ashi no yubi** |
| shoulder(s) | **kata** | ankle(s) | **ashikubi/** |
| spine/ | **sebone** | | **kurubushi** |
| backbone | | heel(s) | **kakato** |
| heart | **shinzō** | | |

## Pains

| | |
|---|---|
| pain | **itami** |
| dull pain | **dontsū** |
| joint pain | **kansetsu no itami** |
| muscle pain | **kinnikutsū** |
| sharp pain | **gekitsū** |
| throbbing pain | **zukizuki suru itami** |
| toothache | **haita** |

コーヒー風呂

コーヒー独特の香りと脂
肪が身体にしみこみお肌
をなめらかにします。

health shop window

## Talking to a doctor or dentist

| | |
|---|---|
| My (stomach) hurts. | **(I) ga itain desu.** |
| I have a (stomach ache). | **(Fukutsū) ga shimasu.** |
| I have an upset stomach. | **Onaka o kowashite imasu.** |
| My (eyes) hurt. | **(Me) ga itain desu.** |
| Am I OK to continue my journey? | **Ryokō wa tsuzuketemo ii desu ka?** |

処方せん
受付ます
平日　9：00～18：00
土曜　9：00～13：00
日・祝　休

prescriptions accepted

## Common symptoms

| | |
|---|---|
| I've been sick. | **Kibun ga waruin desu.** |
| I'm ill with a cold. | **Kaze o hiite imasu.** |
| I feel nauseous. | **Kimochi ga warukute hakisō desu.** |
| I have a sore (throat). | **(Nodo) ga itain desu.** |
| I have a (cough). | **(Seki) ga demasu.** |
| I have a (fever). | **(Netsu) ga arimasu.** |
| I can't feel my (finger/s). | **(Yubi) no kankaku ga arimasen.** |
| I can't move my (neck). | **(Kubi) ga mawarimasen.** |
| I've got (constipation/diarrhoea). | **(Benpi/Geri) o shite imasu.** |
| I have no appetite. | **Shokuyoku ga arimasen.** |

## List of common symptons

Ihara dental clinic

| | |
|---|---|
| back ache | **yōtsū** |
| chills | **samuke/okan** |
| cold | **kaze** |
| constipation | **benpi** |
| diarrhoea | **geri** |
| dizziness | **memai** |
| fever | **netsu** |
| headache | **zutsū** |
| high blood pressure | **kōketsuatsu** |
| indigestion | **shōkafuryō** |
| insomnia | **fuminshō** |
| motion sickness | **norimonoyoi** |
| nausea | **hakike** |
| palpitation(s) | **dōki** |
| rash | **hasshin** |
| shortness of breath | **ikigire** |
| tiredness | **hirō/tsukare** |
| vomit | **ōto/hakukoto** |

# 足元注意

## Watch Your Foot.

## Common accidents

| | |
|---|---|
| I've (cut/burnt) myself. | **(Kega/Yakedo) o shimashita.** |
| I've been bitten by (a dog/an insect). | **(Inu/Mushi) ni kamare mashita.** |
| It hurts here. | **Koko ga itain desu.** |
| I'm allergic to (animals/antibiotics). | **(Dōbutsu/Kōsei bushitsu) niwa arerugii o okoshimasu.** |
| I'm (diabetic/pregnant). | **(Tōnyōbyō/Ninshinchū) desu.** |
| My (daughter/son) has a temperature. | **(Musume/Musuko) ni netsu ga arun desu.** |
| I have a toothache. | **Ha ga itain desu.** |
| I've lost a filling. | **Tsumemono o nakushi mashita.** |

| | |
|---|---|
| **Dō shimashita ka?** | What's wrong with you? |
| **Daijōbu desu.** | You are fine. |
| **Shinpai wa irimasen.** | It's not serious. |
| **Kanja-san wa jūtai desu.** | The patient is in a serious condition. |
| **Hone ga orete imasu.** | The bone is broken. |
| **Shujutsu ga hitsuyō desu.** | You will need an operation. |
| **Taion o hakari masu.** | I'll take your temperature. |
| **Rentogen o torimasu.** | We are going to take an X-ray. |
| **Soko ni yoko ni natte kudasai.** | Please lie down over there. |
| **(Yasumu/Nemuru) hitsuyō ga arimasu.** | You must (rest/sleep). |
| **(Okite/Hashitte/Undō o shite) wa ikemasen.** | You mustn't (get up/run/exercise). |
| **Ashita mata kite kudasai.** | Please come again tomorrow. |
| **O-kusuri o dashimasu kara uketsuke de o-machi kudasai.** | Please wait at reception while we get your medicines ready. |
| **Kari ni tsumete okimasu.** | I'll put in a temporary filling. |
| **Kono ha wa nukanakutewa narimasen.** | I'll have to take this tooth out. |

## Some illnesses

| | |
|---|---|
| appendicitis | **chūsuien/mōchōen** |
| diabetes | **tōnyōbyō** |
| food poisoning | **shokuchūdoku** |
| heart attack | **shinzō hossa** |
| sun stroke | **nesshabyō** |
| hepatitis | **kan(zō)en** |
| pneumonia | **haien** |
| tetanus | **hashōfū** |
| tuberculosis | **kekkaku** |

## At the chemist's

| | |
|---|---|
| Do you have something for (a cold/a cough/a burn/ sunburn/a sting)? | **(Kaze/Seki/Yakedo/Hiyake/ Mushisasare) no kusuri wa arimasu ka?** |
| Do you have any (plasters/ aspirin)? | **(Kattoban /Asupirin) wa arimasu ka?** |
| How should I take this medicine? | **Kono kusuri wa dōyatte nomimasu ka?** |

| | |
|---|---|
| **Kono jōzai o ichijō maishokugo fukuyō shite kudasai.** | Take one tablet after each meal, please. |
| **ichinichi (ikkai/nikai/sankai)** | (once/twice/three times) a day |
| **shokuzen/shokugo** | (before/after) meals |
| **o-mizu to issho ni** | with water |

## Medicines

| | |
|---|---|
| antihistamine | **kō-hisutamin zai** |
| aspirin | **asupirin** |
| cough (medicine/drops) | **sekidome/doroppu** |
| cream | **nankō** |
| eye wash/drops | **megusuri** |
| insulin | **inshurin** |
| laxative | **gezai** |
| medicine | **kusuri** |
| pain killer | **chintsūzai** |
| salve | **nankō** |
| sleeping pill | **suimin'yaku** |
| vitamin(s) | **bitaminzai** |

薬局

## Car breakdown

| | |
|---|---|
| I've broken down. | **Kuruma ga koshō shite shimai mashita.** |
| on the (Tomei) expressway | **(Tōmei) kōsoku dōro de** |
| X kilometres from Y | **Y kara X kiro** |
| The engine won't start. | **Enjin ga kakarimasen.** |
| The (steering wheel) isn't working. | **(Handoru) ga kowarete imasu.** |
| The (brakes) aren't working. | **(Burēki) ga kikimasen.** |
| I've got a (puncture/flat tyre). | **Taiya ga panku shimashita.** |
| I've run out of petrol. | **Gasorin ga arimasen.** |
| When will it be ready? | **Itsu dekimasu ka?** |

## Main car parts

| | | | | |
|---|---|---|---|---|
| accelerator | **akuseru** | | wheels | **hoiiru** |
| brakes | **burēki** | | tyres | **taiya** |
| clutch | **kuratchi** | | windows | **mado** |
| radiator | **rajiēta** | | windscreen | **waipā** |
| steering wheel | **handoru** | | wiper | |

## In the event of an earthquake

| | |
|---|---|
| designated assembly point | **hinanjo** |
| earthquake | **jishin** |
| emergency exit | **hijōguchi** |
| epicentre | **shingenchi** |
| fire | **kaji/kasai** |
| fire extinguisher | **shōkaki** |

避難場所
皇居前広場
Imperial Palace
assembly point

## Theft or loss

| | |
|---|---|
| I've lost my (wallet/passport). | **((O-)saifu/Pasupōto) o nakushi mashita.** |
| My (watch/bag) has been stolen. | **(Ude dokei/Baggu) o nusumare mashita.** |
| yesterday evening/last night/ this morning | **sakuban/sakuya/kesa** |
| in the street/in(side) a store | **michi de/(o-)mise (no naka) de** |

## Valuables and personal belongings

グリーンカウンター
Customer Service Counter
お忘れ物承り所
Lost & Found

| | |
|---|---|
| money | **(o-)kane** |
| wallet/purse | **(o-)saifu** |
| handbag | **handobaggu** |
| briefcase | **buriifukēsu** |
| suitcase | **sūtsukēsu** |
| jewellery | **hōseki/juerii** |
| necklace | **nekkuresu** |
| car | **kuruma** |
| passport | **pasupōto** |
| driving licence | **unten menkyoshō** |
| ticket | **kippu** |

警察
POLICE

| | |
|---|---|
| **Nani o/ga . . . ?** | What . . . ? |
| **Itsu . . . ?** | When . . . ? |
| **Doko de . . . ?** | Where . . . ? |
| **Anata no . . .** | What is your ... |
| **. . . o-namae to jūsho wa (nan desu ka)?** | . . . name and address? |
| **. . . Nihon deno jūsho wa (nan desu ka)?** | . . . address in Japan? |
| **. . . kuruma no nanbā wa (nan desu ka)?** | . . . car registration? |
| **. . . pasupōto bangō wa (nan desu ka)?** | . . . passport number? |
| **Kono yōshi ni kinyū shite kudasai.** | Fill in this form, please. |
| **Ato de kite kudasai.** | Come back later. |
| **(Igirisu taishikan) ni renraku shite kudasai.** | Please inform the (British Embassy). |

lost and found

## Language works

### General

**1** In need of help
☐ **Tasukete! Sumimasen!**
■ **Dō shitan desu ka?**
☐ **Keisatsu o yonde kudasai.**
■ **Hai, wakarimashita.**

Whose help do you need?

### Health

**2** You need an interpreter
☐ **Eigo o hanaseru hito wa imasu ka?**
■ **Hai.**

Did you manage to find anyone who speaks English?

### Talking to a doctor

**3** What's wrong with you?
☐ **Dō shimashita ka?**
■ **Nodo ga itain desu. Seki ga demasu.**
☐ **Hoka ni wa?**
■ **Netsu ga arimasu.**
☐ **Dewa, soko ni yoko ni natte kudasai.**
(**Hoka ni wa?** = Anything else?)

List three symptoms of your condition.
What does the doctor ask you to do?

**4** After an examination
☐ **Shinpai wa irimasen. O-kusuri o dashimasu kara uketsuke de o-machi kudasai.**
■ **Hai.**

The doctor tells you that you need an operation: true/false?

FIRE HYDRANT

消火栓

No. 2423

## At the chemist's

**5** Getting medicine for a cold
☐ **Kaze no kusuri wa arimasu ka?**
■ **Kono jōzai o ichijō maishokugo fukuyō shite kudasai. Ichinichi sankai desu.**
☐ **Hai, wakarimashita.**

The pharmacist instructs you to take these tablets three times a day: true/false?

## Theft or loss

**6** Losing something valuable
☐ **Michi de pasupōto o nakushi mashita.**
■ **Itsu desu ka?**
☐ **Kinō desu.**
■ **Doko de nakushi mashita ka?**
☐ **Wakarimasen . . . doko ka michi de.**
■ **Sō desu ka . . . Dewa kono yōshi ni kinyū shite kudasai.**
(**doko ka michi de** = somewhere on the street)

What questions does the policeman ask you?
What does he then ask you to do?

## Try it out

### Pick one

Which Japanese word, A or B, correctly translates the English?

1 sharp pain
   **A dontsū**      **B gekitsū**
2 toothache
   **A kinnikutsū**  **B haita**
3 doctor
   **A o-isha-san**  **B haisha-san**
4 headache
   **A zutsū**       **B netsu**
5 heart attack
   **A shinzō hossa** **B hakike**
6 burns
   **A rentogen**    **B yakedo**
7 purse/wallet
   **A o-saifu**     **B o-kane**
8 ticket
   **A kippu**       **B kuruma**
9 suitcase
   **A hōseki**      **B sūtsukēsu**
10 earthquake
   **A jishin**      **B shindo**

### As if you were there

Complete your part of the conversations below.

**a** ◻ (My bag has been stolen)
   ■ **Itsu?**
   ◻ (This morning)
   ■ **Doko de?**
   ◻ (I don't know)

**b** ◻ **Dō shimashita ka?**
   ■ (It hurts here)
   ◻ **Rentogen o torimasu.**
   ■ (Am I OK to continue my journey?)
   ◻ **Daijōbu desu. O-daiji ni.**

**c** ◻ (I have a fever. Do you have any aspirin?)
   ■ **Hai, gozaimasu. O-mizu to issho ni nonde kudasai.**

## Sound check

When you see two consonant sounds together, remember to pause briefly after pronouncing the first one.
**Nis san**
**gak kō** (school)
**bag gu** (bag)
**Nip pon** (Japan)
**dorop pu** (cough drops)
**is sho ni** (together with)

Dial 911 for an ambulance or in case of fire

Aoki Dental Clinic

Himawari Chemist's

101

# Doing business

Much has been made over the years about the intricacies of Japanese business protocol; an unintended consequence is that foreign business visitors often anticipate the worst, feel ill at ease, fearing that they will inevitably cause offence and damage business prospects. Short of wanton crassness, such fears are misplaced.

Most Japanese expect non-Japanese visitors to behave differently. To bridge cultural differences, your strategy should include a sensitivity to Japanese comfort factors and a positive, professional approach to interpersonal encounters and the conduct of business relationships. Being attentive to detail, consistent and reliable is not unique to Japan, but are highly regarded qualities which will help overcome differences in approach and business style.

### Key success factors include:

■ doing your homework on the company and on the people you will meet – this shows that you're serious about the relationship and professional in your approach
■ using go-betweens to arrange meetings and anticipate details; these 'fixers' can come from within your organisation or theirs but need to be credible to both sides
■ anticipating what issues your meeting will address and ensuring that you take along appropriate supporting materials. This must

include a quantity of business cards (*meishi*), ideally translated into Japanese (your fixer can be used to help ensure that the translation is accurate – Japanese *meishi* typically focus on your organisational status while Western cards focus more on your job function)
■ dress codes which stress the organisation more than the self. The safest ground involves suits, plain-coloured shirts and sober colours. The Japanese regard style as substance in its own right; your dress is your message. On a practical point, slip-on shoes are easier to get in and out of when visiting restaurants or traditional Japanese buildings where shoes aren't worn
■ using gifts to smooth relationships (see p105).

## Protocol

Procedural protocols are easier to fathom than language protocols. Formality serves two functions in Japanese business: it keeps you at a distance until your Japanese

opposite numbers are comfortable working with you and it reminds everyone that the business you are conducting belongs to the organisation, not to you.

> ❗ I would like to see Mr Yamamoto, Head of the (General Affairs) Department.
> 🔴 **(Sōmubu) no Yamamoto-buchō-san ni ome ni kakari tain desu ga.**

## Meeting comfort factors

■ bow or shake hands with your opposite numbers on arrival, in order of seniority. If you aren't certain about this, allow yourself to be led. If you feel uncomfortable bowing, extend your hand but try to avoid too firm a handshake or too much eye contact; you may find yourself instinctively nodding, which serves as a bow

> ❗ I've come for the (three) o'clock meeting.
> 🔴 **(Sanji) ni ome ni kakaru koto ni natte imasu.**

■ exchange *meishi* (business cards) next. *Meishi* function as a cultural swipe-card; they prove you work for your company, give you a specific hierarchical status and are a useful *aide-mémoire* for remembering names (it's more polite to refer to people by name than by 'you'). *Meishi* are normally studied (briefly) when you receive them, then arranged in (seating) order on the table in front of you when you sit; deftly collecting them up and putting them in your *meishi* holder is a better means of signalling that you have to leave a meeting than glancing at your watch. Don't leave *meishi* behind

> ❗ How do you do? I'm from (ABC). My name's Smith.
> 🔴 **Hajimemashite. (ABC) no (Sumisu) desu.**

■ the use of as much Japanese as you can confidently muster on arrival, when exchanging *meishi* and at the end of your meeting is generally seen as an indication of your sensitivity and your seriousness about the potential relationship

> ❗ I'm pleased to meet you./I look forward to doing business with you.
> 🔴 **Dōzo yoroshiku.**

■ wait to be guided to your seat by the 'fixer'; seating reflects seniority and visitors are generally given the best seats (ie furthest from the door and nearest the window)
■ refreshments are usually provided without first enquiring what your preference is; if you don't like *o-cha* (standard green tea) or *Amerikan kōhii* (weak coffee) it's best to grin and bear it. Leaving food or drink causes no offence in such situations
■ initial meetings, known as *aisatsu* (literally 'greetings') are short and, on the surface at least, insubstantial (limited to an exchange of literature, *meishi*, gifts and small talk). At a deeper level, they reveal the relationship you are there to cultivate – note the level and number of attendees at an *aisatsu* meeting, as this is evidence of how your company and the potential business are perceived
■ body language reveals more than spoken language. Strong eye-contact is avoided since business people do not regard one another as equals (the buyer is stronger than the seller; one company may be larger than the other, the age and

seniority of those present will vary); avoidance equals deference. In a similar vein, juniors will tend to sit closer to the edges of their seats and exhibit more tension in their bodies (body tension = respect). Hands are used less for gesturing (don't point with your fingers) and legs generally not crossed (unless seated on *tatami* mats, where you should avoid 'pointing' your legs at anyone)

■ at your first meeting, you may be offered a gift. It's best to receive it without immediately offering a return gift which you may have brought along; presenting yours at a later stage not only gives your Japanese host centre stage, it also shows you understand the value of understatement and modesty, which are considered signs of confidence and strength

❗ Thank you very much. I'm pleased to receive this.

🔴 **Arigatō gozaimasu. Enryo naku chōdai itashimasu.**

■ uninterrupted monologues are common, especially at set-piece meetings where seniors are present. Where Japanese is the predominant language used, choice of an interpreter and pre-briefing are important. Check first with your hosts to see if they plan to provide an interpreter; if you decide to bring your own, someone from inside your organisation may be viewed more favourably than a professional. It is wise to brief your interpreter in advance on the messages you hope to deliver during the meeting and to suggest how you want your words translated (gist or simultaneously). If you want your words translated more literally, tell your interpreter that you take responsibility for what is said, otherwise they may translate what they feel you meant to say rather than what you actually said. Remember that interpreting is an art, not a science; that being pre-planned, patient and supportive is the best strategy

! Here (is/are) the
document(s) for the
meeting.
**Kaigi no shiryō desu.**

■ frustration or anger
are masked in Japan;
they don't win hearts
and minds. Meetings in
Japan serve a different
purpose and often don't
follow set agenda or
conclude decisively;
think of a meeting as a
substitute for a memo
and you'll get the
picture. Those
attending are often rotated and
seniors (who speak less by virtue of
their status) may nod off, all of
which can be disconcerting to the
unwary. Informal consultations,
known as *nemawashi*, before and
after meetings are used to clarify
issues and resolve differences.

! I'd be grateful if you would read
(this/that).
● **O-yomi itada kereba arigataku
zonji masu.**

# Gifts and gift-giving

Gift-giving highlights the value
placed on reciprocity and mutual
dependence in Japanese society;
debts incurred must be repaid,
favours sought must be preceded by
a visible gesture.

When on business in Japan, don't
just expect to receive gifts, be aware
of little favours done for you which
go beyond the call of duty – these
less obvious 'gifts' should also be
recognised in due course.

Knowing a few principles should
put you at ease; if you're not
comfortable when receiving a gift in
Japan, you can unintentionally
devalue the act of giving and the
giver.

**The basics**
■ gifts are usually wrapped and the
wrapping is considered an intrinsic
part of the gift. Avoid wrapping gifts
yourself, if possible (see Tsutsumu
Factory p45)
■ gifts are generally not opened in
the presence of the giver, but
Japanese have come to expect
Westerners to open theirs
immediately
■ don't exchange gifts
simultaneously. If you are selling,
try to offer your gift first; if you're
beaten to the punch, save yours
until the end of your meeting or
your stay
■ if given a gift, it's generally more
polite to receive it with two hands
and then to raise it slightly. Non-
verbal acts of gratitude like this
generally mean more than words
■ when giving a gift, try to use the
phrase *tsumaranai mono desu ga* ('it's
just a little something') –
understatement reflects well on your
character

! This is a gift from (the UK).
● **(Igirisu) kara no o-miyage desu.**

ラオケ & パーティー
ワイワイ
**OPEN AM 11:30**

■ ideal gifts from foreigners are things which come from your country or region, particularly things not obtainable nor well known in Japan
■ if money is ever given (by you or to you), special printed envelopes should be used. These vary depending on whether the cash is a fare reimbursement, a funeral offering (cash is given to the bereaved) or a wedding present. You can obtain these from stationers and *depāto*, which also have Gift-Giving Advice Centres
■ there are two 'seasons' for gift-giving in Japan: the mid-summer season, *o-chūgen* ( July) and year-end season *o-seibo* (December), when *o-rei* or personal gifts are given to friends and associates. *Kinenhin* or commemorative (often badged) gifts are given at meetings, *o-iwai* are given to celebrate special events (weddings, graduations).

A *wairo* is a bribe or a 'gift' that oversteps the mark.

! Thank you very much for your hospitality today.
● **Kyōwa gochisō sama deshita.**

## Business entertaining

*Settai* (business entertaining) serves many purposes in Japanese society. Since many of the best bars, clubs and restaurants in Japan cater to expense-account customers, *settai* is a perk of working for a corporation

and being a manager. The self-employed, junior staff, part-timers and those working in the 99% of Japanese businesses which employ fewer than 50 people have to pay Japan's high entertainment costs out of their own pockets.

*Settai* also provides a more informal setting and ambience in which to get to know more about the character of your opposite numbers or to conduct business in a more relaxed and private environment; when alcohol is present, discussions are understood to be off-the-record. When privacy is the prime consideration, Japanese will use a *ryōtei* (see p65).

! Not at all, it's my pleasure
**Iie, dō itashimashite.**

*Settai* is not spontaneous; even if you aren't invited until the day of a meeting, arrangements will generally have been made in advance, so anticipate an invitation. If you want to extend one, use your fixer to float the idea in advance. Whoever invites pays for everything. If you are the buyer, ask yourself whether you should be extending an invitation; if you are inviting senior people, choose the club or restaurant with an eye to their status and the value of your business with them, but take local advice on the costs involved too. Remember that in Japan, the prevailing norm is 'there is no free lunch'. As with gift-giving, you are perceived to be investing in the future or repaying a debt from the past. Don't send the wrong signal out of a misguided devotion to etiquette.

! I look forward to continuing our business relationship.
● **Kongo tomo yoroshiku onegai itashimasu.**

# Women in business

Fewer than 3% of Japan's managers are women; the majority of whom work in the service sector (media, fashion, IT, PR/advertising, finance), often in medium-sized businesses. Doing business with corporations, particularly in manufacturing, may mean that there are no women on the Japanese side, apart from interpreters and OLs (office ladies). Sensitivity to Japanese male comfort factors will enhance your effectiveness.

## Male Japanese comfort factors

■ accept honorary male status, if conferred. This is a common solution to the presence of a Western professional woman amidst an all-male Japanese team

■ power-dressing may draw unwanted attention; sober femininity is safest (although pink should be avoided, as it is a sensitive colour in business – it's associated with sex). Heels which cause you to tower over senior Japanese colleagues are inadvisable. Strong fragrances should be avoided by women (and men) doing business in Japan

■ mind your body language. If you opt to bow rather than shake hands,

keep your hands at your sides as you bow (ie as a man would) to differentiate your bow from the customary female bow, in which the hands are placed in front. This will signal that although you are a woman, you are a manager first. During meetings, try to avoid crossing your legs. Avoid embracing or kissing business acquaintances in public

■ accept that some forms of *tsukiai* (socialising) are off-limits to women. Business dinners often take place in the early evening, allowing plenty of time after *settai* has finished for *nijikai* ('the second round') which may not be appropriate for mixed company. You can pre-empt any embarrassment by conveniently having a prior engagement to go to once the *settai* is at an end

■ smoking and drinking by women are acceptable, providing that others are smoking and that you are not drinking anything stronger than your (senior) Japanese opposite numbers. The rule of thumb is not to challenge the Japanese male's self-esteem.

❚ Thank you for your hard work today.
● **Otsukare sama deshita**

# Language builder

Like the Japanese archipelago, the Japanese language stands on its own; it has few parallels with any other group of languages. This makes it a particularly interesting language to learn, because you cannot take anything for granted about its sounds, about how ideas are expressed, how sentences are constructed or how the language is written.

## 'a' and 'the'

Good news here: Japanese has no definite nor indefinite articles.

## Singular and plural

More good news: apart from certain pronouns (I = **watashi**; we = **watashitachi**; this = **kore**; these = **korera**), there are no clearly expressed plurals to worry about. 'A book' or 'some books' is still **hon**; 'a bus' or 'three buses' remains **basu**.

## Genders

The good news continues: Japanese nouns don't have genders, so there's no need to worry about making sure that articles, adjectives, etc agree. Gender only becomes an issue in terms of social contact. For example, in informal situations, men generally use the first-person pronoun **boku**, but women are expected to use **watashi**. When a situation is more formal, both men and women use **watashi**.

## 'Counters'

This is where the good news comes to a bit of a halt. Counting things in Japanese is somewhat complicated because 'counters' must accompany numbers when you specify a quantity in Japanese, and the counters differ when objects have different shapes.

There are, however, two ways of counting things of a generic nature. The one shown here can be used to count up to ten of anything from sweets and packages to fruit and vegetables. The other is to use **-ko**.

| | |
|---|---|
| . . . **hitotsu** | 1 . . . |
| . . . **futatsu** | 2 . . . |
| . . . **mittsu** | 3 . . . |
| . . . **yottsu** | 4 . . . |
| . . . **itsutsu** | 5 . . . |
| . . . **muttsu** | 6 . . . |
| . . . **nanatsu** | 7 . . . |
| . . . **yattsu** | 8 . . . |
| . . . **kokonotsu** | 9 . . . |
| . . . **tō** | 10 . . . |

**-ko**
The counter **-ko** can be used with any small object, from chocolates to eggs, apples to melons.
**tamago ikko** = one egg
**meron niko** = two melons

**-mai**
Used for flat things (eg pictures, photos, paper, shirts, sweaters, bars of chocolate, tickets, stamps)
**ichimai** . . .
**nimai** . . .
**sanmai** . . .
**yonmai** . . . etc

**-satsu**
Used for things with 'pages' (eg books, notebooks, books of tickets)
**issatsu** . . .
**nisatsu** . . .
**sansatsu** . . .
**yonsatsu** . . . etc

**-hon/-pon/-bon**
Used for long, thin objects (eg bottles, ties, films, tapes, cigarettes, pens, pencils, bananas, leeks, carrots, cucumbers)
**ippon** . . .
**nihon** . . .
**sanbon** . . .
**yonhon** . . . etc

**-hiki/-piki/-biki**
Used for fish and small animals (eg cats, dogs, mice, snakes)
**ippiki** . . .
**nihiki** . . .
**sanbiki** . . .
**yonhiki** . . . etc

**-wa/-ba**
Used for birds and rabbits
**ichiwa** . . .
**niwa** . . .
**sanwa/sanba** . . .
**yonwa** . . . etc

**-hai/-pai/-bai**
Used for glasses of drinks
**ippai** . . .
**nihai** . . .
**sanbai** . . .
**yonhai** . . . etc

Don't worry too much about choosing the correct counter. Most Japanese will still understand if you use a cardinal number.

## Saying 'you'

There are different ways to say things in Japanese depending on the social context in which you find yourself. For this reason, there are several different ways to say 'you', but generally speaking, the Japanese prefer the use of names (eg **Yamamoto-san**) or role titles (eg **sensei** when speaking to a doctor) because 'you' feels somewhat distant or impersonal to a Japanese speaker. Note that **san** is a neutral mark of respect added at the end of a person's name (either first name or surname). It can be used for all adults, regardless of social/marital status, age or gender.

The most commonly used form of 'you' is **anata**; if you are a senior person speaking to a junior, you could use **kimi**; if a man is trying to be impolite to make a point, he would use **omae**.

## Missing words: subjects

Japanese speakers often omit the subject of their sentences, unless they want to emphasise a point or if the subject wouldn't otherwise be clear from the context of the sentence.

**Watashi wa tsukare mashita.**
I'm tired. (spoken by a foreigner or to emphasise that *you're* tired, not someone else)
**Tsukare mashita.** I'm tired. (more natural sounding)

Omitting the subject gives a natural feel to a Japanese speaker. It is perfectly acceptable for foreigners to include subjects when they speak, but it does mark them out as non-native speakers.

## Word order

Generally speaking, what comes later in a Japanese sentence is more important than what comes at the beginning. The basic structure of Japanese is:
**subject – object – verb**
For example, 'It's Wednesday today' in Japanese is:
**Kyō** (Today)
**wa** (subject indicator)
**Suiyōbi** (Wednesday)
**desu** (is)

'I/we eat/will eat a/some satsuma/s' in Japanese is:
**Mikan**        satsuma(s)
**o**        object indicator
**tabemasu**        eat/will eat

Note that in the last sentence, the object appears to come first because the subject is missing (see Missing words).

**Wa** or **ga** after the subject of a Japanese sentence is a part of speech known as a 'subject indicator'; **o** after the object of a sentence is known as an 'object indicator'; these are helpful in clarifying the function of nouns within a Japanese sentence.

## Personal pronouns

| I | watashi | wa/ga |
|---|---|---|
| you | anata/kimi | wa/ga |
| he | kare | wa/ga |
| she | kanojo | wa/ga |
| we | watashitachi | wa/ga |
| they | karera | wa/ga |

| my | watashi no |
|---|---|
| your | anata/kimi no |
| his | kare no |
| her | kanōjo no |
| our | watashitachi no |
| their | karera no |

| me | watashi ni |
|---|---|
| you | anata/kimi ni |
| him | kare ni |
| her | kanojo ni |
| us | watashitachi ni |
| them | karera ni |

## Tense

The expression of tenses is not complicated in Japanese. There are essentially three types of tense in Japanese verbs:

- present and simple future tenses
  **Mikan o (tabemasu).**
  [subject] (eat(s)/will eat) (a) satsuma(s).
- continuous present
  **Mikan o (tabete imasu).**
  [subject] (is/are eating) (a) satsuma(s).
- past, present perfect and past perfect
  **Mikan o (tabe mashita).**
  [subject] (ate/has/have/had eaten) (a) satsuma(s).

## Asking questions

By adding **ka** to the end of a verb, you change it into a question. For example:
**Kyō wa Suiyōbi desu <u>ka</u>?**
Is it Wednesday today?

## Negatives

By changing the verb ending to **sen**, sentences become negative. For example:
**Mikan o tabemasen.**
I don't eat satsumas.
**Mikan o tabete imasen.**
I'm not eating satsumas.
**Mikan o tabemasen deshita.**
I didn't eat/have/had not eaten satsumas.

(**Deshita** indicates the past tense.)

The verb **desu** (to be) is conjugated to **dewa arimasen**.

## Which one?

There are different ways to say 'this/that' depending on how close the object you are referring to is to you. For example:
**kore** is used for something which is close to you. It means 'this'.
**sore** is used for something which is closer to the listener. It means 'that'.
**are** is used for something which is not close to you nor to the listener. It means 'that (one) over there'.
**dore** means 'which'.
**koko** means 'here'.
**soko** means 'there'.
**asoko** means 'over there'.

# Answers

## Bare necessities

1 Yes; in the morning  2 Yes

**Line up**
1 e  2 f  3 d  4 b  5 a  6 c

**A date for your diary**
a Ichigatsu Jūgonichi  b Gogatsu
Mikka  c Shichigatsu Hatsuka  d
Jūgatsu Tōka  e Jūnigatsu
Nijūsannichi

## Getting around

1 true  2 Go straight on; false
3 true  4 platform 12  5 an hour
6 take a taxi

**Mix and match**
1 e  2 f  3 g  4 a  5 d  6 c  7 b

**Fill the gaps**
oshiete kudasai; shingō; migi;
hidari; Dōmo arigatō/
Sumimasen

## Somewhere to stay

1 For how many people?; For how
many nights?  2 to repeat your
name  3 7 am and 10 am; you
get an outside line  4 false
5 Have you used the minibar?

**Key words**
1 hoteru  2 yūsu hosuteru  3
terebi  4 resutoran  5 hōmu sutei
6 eakon  7 koin randorii  8 o-
furo/basurūmu  9 kii/kagi

**As if you were there**
■ Konnichiwa. Yoyaku o shita
[your surname] desu.
■ Chōshoku wa nanji desu ka?
■ Resutoran wa doko ni arimasu
ka?
■ Heya wa nangai ni arimasu ka?

■ Erebētā wa arimasu ka?
■ Arigatō/Dōmo arigatō/Dōmo
sumimasen.

## Buying things

1 Yes; ¥200  2 8 pm; 5th floor
3 true; false  4 true; false  5 one
bag  6 tomorrow afternoon
7 ¥70; fill in a form

**Going shopping**
a Kurisumasu kādo o nitsū
kudasai.
b Fuirumu o nihon kudasai.
c Batterii o sanko kudasai.
d ¥70 (Nanajū-en) kitte o yonmai
kudasai.
e Kōkū shokan o rokutsū
kudasai.
f Ichigo o hitohako kudasai.
g Hamu o nihyaku guramu
kudasai.

## Café life

1 ham, egg and cheese
sandwiches; coffee, tea and hot
chocolate  2 true  3 at the till

**Snack time**
a hotto kēki to kōhii (a pancake
@ ¥550 and a coffee @ ¥450)
b orenji jūsu to kurēpu (an
orange juice ¥800 and a crèpe
¥400)
c kapuchiino to tōsuto (a
cappuccino @ ¥500 and toast
@ ¥380)
d jin tonikku to hotto doggu (a
gin and tonic – the only
alcoholic drink listed) and a
hot dog @ ¥350)

**Where to go?**
a kakuteru bā/raunji bā
b biya gāden
c karaoke bā

# Eating out

1 Do you have a reservation?
2 yes; yes 3 steak, rare;
Japanese tea 4 plum wine; they
don't have any; false 5 How do
you eat this?; Would you like
anything else? 6 credit card; yes

### Odd one out
a pan (the others are all noodles)
b supagetti (the others are all
forms of bread) c Nihoncha (the
others are all beers)

### At the table
1 (o-)hashi 2 fōku 3 naifu
4 (tēburu) napukin 5 (o-)saji/
supūn 6 (o-)shio 7 koshō

### As if you were there
a Kono chikaku ni ii resutoran
wa arimasu ka?
b Futari onegai shimasu.
c Kyō no sūpu wa nan desu ka?
d Tenpura ni shimasu./Tenpura
o onegai shimasu.
e Atsukan ippon kudasai.
f Kore wa dōyatte taberun desu
ka?
g Oishikatta desu.

# Entertainment and leisure

1 one-day or half-day; (a)
brochure/s 2 no 3 (a)
programme/s; yes (of 20
minutes) 4 baseball and sumō;
no

### Name it
1 o-shiro 2 Nihon teien 3 kōen
4 jinja 5 o-tera

### Mix and match
1 d 2 a 3 e 4 b 5 c

### As if you were there
a Chiketto wa arimasu ka?

b Kono seki wa aite imasu ka?
c Hokkaido de sukii o shitain
desu ga.

# Emergencies

1 police 2 yes 3 sore throat,
cough, fever; lie down there
4 false 5 true 6 when did you
lose it?, where did you lose it?;
fill in a form

### Pick one
1 B 2 B 3 A 4 A 5 A 6 B 7 A
8 A 9 B 10 A

### As if you were there
a ☐ Baggu o nusumare mashita.
  ☐ Kesa desu.
  ☐ Wakarimasen.
b ■ Koko ga itain desu.
  ■ Ryokō wa tsuzuketemo ii
  desu ka?
c ☐ Netsu ga arimasu. Asupirin
  wa arimasu ka?

# Dictionary

(see also Menu reader, p76)

**achira** over there/that way
**ago** chin, jaw
**Ainu** original inhabitants of Japan in Hokkaidō
**airon** iron
**aisatsu** greeting
**aisu kōhii** iced coffee
**aisu tii** iced tea
**aisukuriimu** ice-cream
**aiteiru/aku** to be free, vacant, open
**aka** red
**akachōchin** Japanese-style pub with red lanterns
**akuseru** accelerator
**akusesarii** accessory
**amakuchi** sweet (sake or wine)
**amari . . . de nai** not really/not very much
**annaijo** information desk
**anzu** apricot
**ao** blue
**apāto** apartment, flat
**are** that one over there
**arerugii** allergy
**arigatō** thanks, thank you
**aru** to have/exist
**arukōru** alcohol
**asa** morning
**ashi** leg, foot
**ashi no yubi** toe
**ashikubi** ankle
**ashita/asu** tomorrow
**asoko** over there
**asuparagasu** asparagus
**asupirin** aspirin
**atama** head
**atatakai** warm
**ato de** later, after
**atsukan** warmed sake
**azukaru** to look after (belongings)

**bā** bar
**bāgen** bargain
**baggu** bag
**baiten** kiosk, small shop
**banana** banana
**bangō** number
**barē** ballet
**barēbōru** volleyball
**basu** bus
**basu tsuā** bus tour
**basutei** bus stop
**bengoshi** lawyer
**benpi** constipation
**bentō/o-bentō** boxed lunch
**biiru** beer
**bijinesu hoteru** business hotel
**bijutsukan** art gallery
**binmei** flight number
**bitaminzai** vitamin tablets
**biya gāden** beer garden
**bōi/bōi-san** waiter
**bon/o-bon** festival of the dead
**bōringujō** bowling alley
**bōringu** ten-pin bowling
**bōru** ball
**budō** grape
**bunbōgu** stationery
**bunraku** puppet theatre
**burandē** brandy
**burausu** blouse
**burēki** brake
**buriifukēsu** briefcase
**būtsu** boots
**byōin** hospital

**cha-no-yu** tea ceremony
**cha/o-cha** Japanese green tea
**chairo** brown
**chawan/o-chawan** rice bowl
**chekku auto** check-out
**chekku in** check-in
**chiisai** small
**chiizu** cheese
**chika/chikai** basement
**chikai** near, close
**chikaku ni** nearby
**chikatetsu** tube, underground
**chiketto** ticket
**chintsūzai** painkiller
**chizu** map
**chō** intestine

**chōdo** exact
**chokorēto** chocolate
**chōshoku** breakfast
**chotto** a little
**chūsha ryōkin** parking fee
**chūshoku** lunch
**chūsuien** appendicitis

**daburu** double (room)
**daibingu** diving
**daidokoro** kitchen
**daigaku** university
**daijōbu(na)** fine/all right
**danbō** heating
**deguchi** exit
**dekakeru** to leave
**dekiru** to be able to
**denchi** battery
**denki-ya** electrical shop
**denkyū** light bulb
**densha** train
**denwa o kakeru** to telephone
**denwa ryōkin** telephone charge
**depāto** department store
**deru** to exit
**dezāto** dessert
**disuko** disco
**doa** door
**dōbutsu** animal
**dōbutsuen** zoo
**dōgu** tool, equipment
**dōki** palpitations
**doko?** where?
**doku** to go away
**dokushin** single/unmarried
**dōmo** hi/sorry/thanks
**dono gurai/kurai** how much?
**dontsū** dull pain
**dorai kuriiningu** dry cleaning
**doraiyā** hairdryer
**dore?** which?
**doresshingu** salad dressing
**Doyōbi** Saturday
**dōzo** please

**eakon** air-conditioning
**ebi** shrimp
**ehagaki** picture postcard
**eigakan** cinema
**Eigo** English
**eigyōbu** sales department

**eigyōchū** in business, operation
**Eiji shinbun** English newspaper
**eki** station
**engeijō** vaudeville theatre
**enjin** engine
**enkaijō** party room
**enki** postponement
**erebētā** lift, elevator
**esukarētā** escalator
**fasuto fūdo** fast food
**fōku** fork
**fuirumu** film (photo)
**fujin** lady
**fujinfuku** ladies' wear
**fukubu** abdomen
**fukuro** bag
**fukutsū** stomach ache
**fuminshō** insomnia
**fun** minute
**funabin** sea-mail
**fun'iki no ii** having good
atmosphere
**furo/o-furo** bath, bathroom
**furonto** reception desk (hotel)
**furui** old
**furūtsu** fruit
**fūsho** letter
**futari** two people
**futsū** normal, standard
**futsū densha** local service train

**gagaku** classical court music
**gaido tsuki no** guided
**gaiji** external ear
**gaijin** foreigner
**gaikokujin** foreigner
**gaisen** outside telephone line
**gakkō** school
**gakusei** student
**garō** gallery
**gasorin** petrol
**gasorin sutando** petrol station
**gekijō** theatre
**gekitsū** sharp pain
**gengō** regnal dating system
**genki(na)** healthy, well
**genkin** cash
**geri** diarrhoea
**geta** wooden clogs
**gezai** laxative
**ginkō** bank

**ginkōin** bank worker
**gin'iro** silver
**gochisōsama** thank you for the food (after eating)
**gofujin** Ladies (toilet)
**gogo** afternoon
**gohan** steamed rice
**gōkei de** in total
**gomen nasai** (I'm) sorry
**gorufu** golf
**gorufu renshūjō** golf range
**gorufujō** golf course
**goyukkuri** enjoy yourself/make yourself at home
**gozen** morning
**gurai** about
**guramu** gramme
**gurasu** glass
**gurēpufurūtsu** grapefruit
**guriin piisu** pea
**guriinsha** green car (first-class carriage)

**ha** tooth
**hagaki** postcard
**hai** yes
**haien** pneumonia
**haiiro** grey
**haikanryō** entry fee for shrines and temples
**haita** toothache
**hajimemashite** how do you do
**hakike** nausea
**hakobu** to carry (something)
**haku** to be sick, vomit
**hakubutsukan** museum
**hana** flower/nose
**hanabi taikai** fireworks display
**hanaseru** to be able to speak
**hanasu** to speak
**handobaggu** handbag
**handoru** steering wheel
**hangaku** half-price
**hannichi** half-day
**harau** to pay
**hashi** bridge
**hashi/o-hashi** chopsticks
**hashiru** to run
**hashōfū** tetanus
**hasshin** rash
**hayai** early/quick

**heiten** to close a shop (for a day/forever)
**heiten jikan** closing time (for a shop)
**heya** room
**hidari** left
**hidarite ni** on your left
**higashi** east
**hiji** elbow
**hijōguchi** emergency exit
**hikōjō** airport
**hikōki** aeroplane
**hinanjo** assembly point (in case of disaster)
**hirō** tiredness
**hito** person
**hitori** one person
**hitsuyō(na)** necessary
**hiyake** sunburn
**hiyazake** cold/unheated sake
**hiza** knee(s)
**hoiiru** wheel
**hōmon** visit
**hōmonsuru** to visit
**hōmu sutei** homestay (a stay with a family in a foreign country)
**hon-ya** book shop
**hone** bone
**honjitsu** today
**hōrensō** spinach
**hōseki** jewellery
**hoshii** to want
**hoteru** hotel
**hotto** hot
**hotto doggu** hot dog

**i** stomach
**ichiban** best, first, most
**ichigo** strawberry
**ichiman** 10,000
**ichinichi** one day
**ie** home, house
**Igirisu** the UK
**ii** good
**iie** no
**ikebana** flower arranging
**ikigire** shortness of breath
**ikkai** ground floor/once
**iku** to go
**ikura** how much? (cost)
**ikutsu?** how many?

**inshurin** insulin
**intābaru** interval
**inu** dog
**ippaku** one-night stay
**ippon** one bottle/pen (counter)
**iriguchi** entrance
**irochigai** different colour
**irrashaimase** welcome, hello/may I help you?
**isha/o-isha-san** doctor
**isogashii** busy
**isshiki** one set
**isshoni** together
**itadakimasu** thank you for the food (before eating)
**itami** pain
**itsu?** when?
**iu** to say
**izakaya** pub

**jagaimo** potato
**jaguchi** tap
**jaketto** jacket
**jikan** time
**jikokuhyō** timetable
**jin tonikku** gin and tonic
**jinja** shrine
**jinjāēru** ginger ale
**jinzō** kidney
**jishin** earthquake
**jitensha** bicycle
**jiyūseki** non-reserved seat
**jōhō** information
**jōhō shakai** information society
**jōhōshi** entertainment guide
**jokkii** big mug for beer
**jōzai** pill/tablet (medicine)
**jūsho** address
**jūsu** juice
**jūtai** serious illness/traffic jam

**ka** ? (makes a sentence interrogative)
**kādigan** cardigan
**kado** corner
**kādo** card (often credit card)
**kaesu** to give back, hand over
**kafe** cafe
**kagi** key
**kagu** to smell
**kagu** furniture

**kaidan** stairs
**kaigan** beach
**kaigi** meeting
**kaikei** cash register
**kaisatsuguchi** ticket barrier
**kaishain** company employee
**kaisui pantsu** bathing suit (men)
**kaisuiyoku** swimming in the sea
**kaiten** open for business (shop)
**kaiten jikan** opening time (for a shop)
**kaiten zushi** sushi fast food style served on a carousel
**kaitensuru** to rotate
**kaji** fire
**kakaru** to take (time, money)
**kakato** heel
**kaki** persimmon
**kakuteru bā** cocktail bar
**kamareru** to be bitten
**kami** hair/paper
**kaminoke** hair
**kamo shirenai** maybe
**kan(zō)en** hepatitis
**kane/o-kane** money
**kangaeru** to think (about)
**kanja/kanja-san** patient
**kanji** Chinese character
**kanjō/o-kanjō** bill
**kankaku** feeling (not numbness)
**kankō** sightseeing
**kankō annaijo** tourist information
**kanpai!** cheers!
**kansetsu no itami** pain in the joints
**kanzō** liver
**kao** face
**kapuseru hoteru** capsule hotel
**kara** from
**kara(no)** empty
**karada** body
**karakuchi** dry (sake/wine)
**karashi** mustard
**karifurawā** cauliflower
**kariru** to borrow
**kasai** fire
**kata** shoulder
**katamichi** one-way
**kattoban** plaster (for cuts)
**kau** to buy

**kawa** river
**kaze** cold (illness)/wind
**kaze o hiku** to catch a cold
**kazoku** family
**kechappu** ketchup
**kega** injury
**keiba** horse racing
**keibajō** racecourse
**keikan** police officer
**keisatsu** police
**keishoku** snack
**kēki** cake
**kekkaku** tuberculosis
**kekkon** marriage
**kekkō(na)** fine
**ken** ticket
**ken'eki** quarantine
**kesa** this morning
**keshōshitsu** powder room
**ki o tsukete!** take care!
**kibun** health, well-being
**kichōhin** valuables
**kii** key
**kiiro** yellow
**kikinzoku** jewellery
**kimaru** to be decided
**kimeru** to decide
**kimochi** ambience, feeling
**kinkyū(no)** urgent
**kinnikutsū** muscle pain
**kinō** yesterday
**kinyūsuru** to fill in (form)
**kin'en** non-smoking
**kin'iro** gold
**kiosuku** kiosk
**kippu** ticket
**kippu uriba** ticket office/counter
**kiro** kilogramme, kilometre
**kissaten** coffee shop
**kita** north
**kitsuen** smoking
**kitte** stamp
**kōban** police box
**kochira** this way
**kodomo** child
**kōen** park
**kōhii shoppu** coffee shop
**kōishitsu** changing room
**kōka** coin
**kōketsuatsu** high blood pressure

**koko** here
**kokoa** cocoa
**kōkū shokan** aerogramme
**kōkūbin** air-mail
**kōkūgaisha** airline company
**kokugo** Japanese language
**kokusan** domestically produced
**kōkyo** Imperial palace
**kōkyū resutoran** high-class restaurant
**kōmuin** public servant
**konbanwa** hello (good evening)
**konnichiwa** hello (good afternoon)
**konsāto** concert
**koppu** glass (for water)
**kōra** cola
**kore** this
**koori** ice
**kōsei bushitsu** antibiotics
**koshi** hips/lower back
**koshō** pepper
**koshōsuru** to break down (car/machine)
**kōshū denwa** public telephone
**kōsoku dōro** expressway
**kōto** coat
**koto** stringed musical instrument
**kowasu** to break
**kozara** small plate
**kozutsumi** parcel
**kubi** neck
**kuchi** mouth
**kūkō** airport
**kurai** about
**kuratchi** clutch
**kurejitto kādo** credit card
**kuro** black
**kurōku** cloakroom
**kuru** to come (from)
**kuruma** car
**kusuri** medicine
**kusuri-ya** chemist, pharmacy
**kutsu** shoe
**kutsushita** sock
**kuyakusho** ward office
**kyabetsu** cabbage
**kyaku/o-kyaku-sama** customer
**kyanpujō** campsite
**kyanserusuru** to cancel
**kyō** today

**kyōgen** traditional comic play
**kyōshi** teacher
**kyūkei** interval, break
**kyūkō** express train
**kyūkyūsha** ambulance
**kyūri** cucumber

**machigai** mistake
**made** to
**mado** window
**magaru** to turn
**maiko** apprentice geisha/dancer
**makaseru/o-makasesuru** to
leave it up to someone
**makura** pillow
**manseki** full up (no seats
remaining)
**manshitsu** no vacancies (hotel)
**masshurūmu** mushroom
**massugu(na)** straight
**masutādo** mustard
**mata** again
**matsu** to wait
**matsuri** festival
**mawaru** to turn, rotate
**mayonēzu** mayonnaise
**me** eye
**megusuri** eye medicine
**meibutsu** speciality
**mein kōsu** main course
**meishi** business card
**memai** dizziness
**menyū** menu
**meron** melon
**mētoru** metre
**mezamashi dokei** alarm clock
**midori** green
**mieru** to be able to see
**migi** right
**migite ni** on your right
**miidiamu** medium
**mikado** emperor
**mikan** satsuma
**mimi** ear
**minami** south
**mineraru uōta** mineral water
**minibā** minibar
**minshuku** inn (B&B style)
**miri mētoru** millimetre
**miri rittoru** millilitre
**miru** to see

**miruku** milk
**mise/o-mise** shop
**miseru** to show
**miyage/o-miyage** souvenir
**miyagehinten** souvenir shop
**mizu/o-mizu** water
**mizugi** bathing suit (women)
**mizuumi** lake
**mizuwari** whisky and water
**mōchōen** appendicitis
**mōfu** blanket
**mōichido** again
**mokuteki** aim, purpose
**momo** peach/thigh
**mōningu kōru** wake-up call
**mōshikomisho** application form
**mōshikomu** to apply (for)
**mōshiwake gozaimasen** (I'm)
very sorry (formal)
**moyooshimono kaijō** event hall
**mugicha** buckwheat tea
**mune** chest (body)
**murasaki** purple
**muryō** free of charge
**mushi** insect
**mushoku** out of work/no work
**musuko** son
**musume** daughter
**myūjikaru** musical

**nagame** view
**naifu** knife
**naiji** inner ear
**naitā** night game (baseball)
**nama biiru** draft beer
**namae** name
**nan . . . ?** what . . . ?
**nangai?** which floor?
**nani?** what?
**nanji?** what time?
**nankō** cream (medicine)
**nanmei?** how many people?
**nanpaku?** how many nights?
**nansai?** how old?
**nashi** pear
**negi** leek
**nekkuresu** necklace
**nekutai** tie
**nemuru** to sleep
**nesshabyō** sun-stroke
**netsu** fever

**nihaku** two-nights' stay
**Nihon buyō** Japanese dance
**Nihon teien** Japanese garden
**Nihongo** Japanese
**Nihonjin** Japanese person
**Nihonshu** sake
**nijikai** second party/second round
**nikai** first floor
**niku/o-niku** meat
**nimotsu** luggage
**ninjin** carrot
**ninshin** pregnancy
**nishi** west
**niwa** garden
**nodo** throat
**Noh** Noh theatre, play
**nomihōdai** all-you-can-drink
**nomimono** drink
**nomu** to drink
**non-sumōkingu** non-smoking
**norimonoyoi** motion sickness
**nurukan** slightly warmed sake
**nusumareru** to have stolen
**nyūjōken** ticket (for concert/play)
**nyūjōryō** admission fee
**nyūkoku kādo** disembarkation card
**nyūkoku shinsa** passport control

**ōfuku** return (ticket)
**ohayō gozaimasu** good morning
**oiru** oil
**oishii** delicious
**okashii** strange, not right, funny
**ōkii** large
**okiru** to get up
**okujō** roof (accessible)
**okureru** to be late
**okuru** to send
**okusan/okusama** (your) wife
**omedetō gozaimasu** congratulations
**omoshiroi** interesting
**on za rokku** on the rocks (drinks)
**onaka** belly
**onegai shimasu** please
**onsen** spa
**opera** opera
**orenji** orange
**osaki ni** ahead of (someone)

**oshieru** to tell, teach
**o-susume** recommendation
**ōto** vomiting
**otona** adult (person)
**owaru** to end
**oyayubi** thumb
**oyogu** to swim

**pachinko** pinball game
**painappuru** pineapple
**pajama** pyjamas
**pan** bread
**pan-ya** bakery
**panfuretto** pamphlet
**panku** puncture
**pantsu** ladies' trousers
**pasupōto** passport
**piiman** green pepper
**pondo** pound sterling
**pun(fun)** minute
**purei gaido** play guide
**purezento** present, gift
**purinto** print (photo)
**puroguramu** programme (theatre, concert, musical)
**pūru** swimming pool

**rabu hoteru** love hotel
**raisu** rice
**rajiētā** radiator
**rajio** radio
**raketto** racket
**rakugo** traditional story-telling
**rappingu** wrapping
**raunji bā** lounge bar
**reinkōto** raincoat
**reishu** cold, unheated sake
**reji** cash register
**remon** lemon
**renrakusuru** to contact, to connect
**rentakā** rental car
**rentogen** X-ray
**reshiito** receipt
**ressun** lesson
**resutoran** restaurant
**retasu** lettuce
**retsu** row (of seats)/queue
**rikon** divorce
**rikyūru** liqueur
**ringo** apple

**rittoru/rittā** litre
**rotenburo** outdoor bath
**roze** rosé wine
**rūmu sābisu** room service
**ryōgae** currency exchange
**ryōgaejo** bureau de change
**ryokan** Japanese style inn
**ryōkin** fare
**ryōkinhyō** tariff
**ryokō** journey
**ryōri** food, cuisine
**ryōshūsho** receipt
**ryōtei** high-class Japanese restaurant

**sābisu no ii** good service
**sābisuryō** service charge
**sāfin** surfing
**sāfubōdo** surfboard
**sagasu** to look for
**saifu** wallet/purse
**saikuringu** cycling
**sain** signature
**saishokushugi-sha** vegetarian
**saishū** last service (bus, train)
**saizu** size
**saji/o-saji** spoon
**sakana/o-sakana** fish
**sakazuki** tiny sake cup
**sakkā** soccer
**sakkājō** soccer pitch
**sakuban** yesterday evening
**sakuya** last night
**samete iru** to be cold
**sandoitchi** sandwich
**sara/o-sara** plate
**sarariiman** business man, company employee
**satō/o-satō** sugar
**sayōnara** goodbye
**sebiro** suit
**sebone** spine
**seki** cough/seat
**sekidome** cough medicine
**sekken** soap
**semai** small, narrow
**senaka** one's back
**senbei/o-senbei** rice cracker
**senchi** centimetre
**sentō** public bath house
**serori** celery

**sēru** sale
**serufu sābisu** self-service
**sērusuman** sales person
**sētā** sweater
**settai** business entertaining
**setto** set meal
**shashin** photograph
**shashin-ya** photography shop
**shawā** shower
**shayōzoku** businessman with expense account
**shichakusuru** to try on (clothes)
**shichimi** spicy Japanese pepper
**shigoto** work
**shiharau** to pay
**shihei** banknote
**shii shii** cc/centilitre
**shinbun** newspaper
**shingō** traffic lights
**shingu** bedding
**shinguru** single (room)
**shinshifuku** menswear
**shinzō** heart
**shinzō hossa** heart attack
**shio/o-shio** salt
**shiri/o-shiri** buttocks
**shiro/o-shiro** castle
**shiro(i)** white
**shiryō** document
**shita** below/tongue
**shiteiseki** reserved seat
**shizuka(na)** quiet
**shōbōsha** fire brigade
**shōchū** rice liqueur
**shōgun** military supremo
**shōjin ryōri** traditional Buddhist vegetarian food
**shōkafuryō** indigestion
**shōkaki** fire extinguisher
**shokuchūdoku** food poisoning
**shokudō** canteen/oesophagus
**shokuji tsuki** dinner included
**shokuryōhin** foodstuffs
**shokuyoku** appetite
**shoten** book shop
**shōyu/o-shōyu** soy sauce
**shufu** housewife
**shujutsu** operation
**shukkoku** embarkation
**shukubō** temple lodging
**shūten** terminus

**shūyūken** excursion ticket
**sofuto dorinku** soft drink
**sokkusu** socks
**soko** there
**sokutatsu** express (mail)
**sore** it/that
**sōsu** brown sauce
**su/o-su** vinegar
**sugu ni** straight away/soon
**suiei** swimming
**suijō sukii** water skiing
**suijō takushii** water taxi
**suimin'yaku** sleeping pill
**suisen** recommendation
**suizō** pancreas
**sukasshu** squash (sport)
**suki** to like, to be fond of
**sukii** skiing
**sukii gerende** ski slope
**sukii gutsu** ski boots
**sukiijō** ski resort
**sukoshi** a little
**sumimasen** excuse me, sorry, thank you
**sunakku** snack bar (expensive pub)
**sunōbōdo** snow-board
**sūpu** soup
**supūn** spoon
**suraido** slide (photo)
**surippa** slippers
**susumeru** to recommend
**sutēki** steak
**sūtsu** suit
**sūtsukēsu** suitcase
**suu** to smoke/to inhale

**tabako** cigarette
**tabako o suu** to smoke a cigarette
**tabehōdai** all-you-can-eat
**taberu** to eat
**tadaima** now/I'm back/I'm home
**taion** body temperature
**taishikan** embassy
**taishoku** retirement
**taiya** tyre
**taizai** stay
**takai** expensive/high, tall
**taki** waterfall

**takushii noriba** taxi rank
**tamago** egg
**tamanegi** onion
**tanoshimu** to have fun, to enjoy
**taoru** towel
**tasukeru** to help
**tatami** straw matting
**taun mappu** town plan
**te** hand
**tēburu napukin** serviette
**tegami** letter
**teijiro** T-junction
**teikyūbi** regular closing day (for shops, restaurants)
**teishoku** set menu/meal
**tēma pāku** theme park
**tenimotsu azukarijo** left-luggage
**tenisu** tennis
**tenjōin** tour attendant
**tenrankai** exhibition
**tera/o-tera** temple
**tōi** far
**toire** toilet
**tōjitsu** on the day specified
**tōjō jikan** boarding time
**tokei** clock
**tokkuri** sake carafe
**tokkyū** special express train
**tokubetsu(na)** special
**tomaru** to stop, to stay
**tomato** tomato
**tōmorokoshi** (sweet) corn
**tonogata** Gents (toilet)
**tōnyōbyō** diabetes
**toraberāzu chekku** travellers' cheque
**toru** to take (photo, object)
**toshokan** library
**tozan** mountain climbing
**tsuā** tour
**tsugi** next
**tsuika ryōkin** surcharge
**tsuin** twin (room)
**tsukare** tiredness
**tsukareru** to become tired
**tsukau** to use
**tsuki** included, moon
**tsuma** (my) wife
**tsume** nail
**tsumemono** filling (tooth)
**tsumetai** cold

**tsuri/o-tsuri** change (money)
**tsuri** fishing
**tsūro** aisle
**tsutsumi** package
**tsutsumu** to wrap up
**tsūyaku** interpreter
**tsūyakusuru** to interpret
**tsuzukeru** to continue

**ude** arm
**ude dokei** wrist watch
**ue** above
**ueitā** waiter
**uisukii** whisky
**ukeru** to receive/take (lesson)
**umeshu** sweet plum wine
**undō o suru** to exercise
**unten menkyoshō** driving licence
**uriba** place where things are sold
**urikire** sold out

**wafū** Japanese style
**wain bā** wine bar
**waipā** windscreen wiper
**wairo** bribe
**waishatsu** shirt
**wakaru** to understand
**wan/o-wan** Japanese soup bowl
**waribiki ryōkin** discount rate
**warikan** sharing costs
**warimashi ryōkin** surcharge
**warui** bad
**wasabi** Japanese green mustard
**washitsu** Japanese-style room
**washoku** Japanese cuisine
**wasureru** to forget
**watashi** I
**watashitachi** we

**yakedo** burn
**yakkyoku** chemist, pharmacy
**yakuza** Japanese underworld gangs
**yakyū** baseball
**yakyūjō** baseball ground
**yama nobori** mountain climbing
**yasai** vegetable
**yasui** cheap
**yasumu** to rest
**yōbi** day of the week
**yobu** to call (somebody, taxi)

**yoi** good
**yoko** side
**yoko ni naru** to lie down
**yoku** often
**yokujō** communal bath
**Yōroppa** Europe
**yoroshii** OK, good
**yoru** night
**yose** traditional storytellers' hall
**yōshi** form/paper
**yōshitsu** Western-style
**yōshoku** Western food
**yotei** plan, intention
**yōtsū** backache
**yoyaku** reservation
**yubi** finger
**yūbinkyoku** post office
**yūenchi** playground
**yūgata** evening
**yukata** Japanese cotton robe
**yuki** to, bound for
**yuki matsuri** snow festival
**yukidomari** dead end
**yukkuri** slowly
**yūkō** valid
**yūmei(na)** famous
**yunyū** import
**yūryō** charged
**yūshoku** dinner
**yūsu hosuteru** youth hostel

**zaseki** seat
**zeikan** customs (and excise)
**zeikin** tax
**zeikomi** tax included
**zenbu** all
**zensai** starter
**zōri** Japanese-style sandal
**zubon** trousers
**zukizukisuru itami** throbbing pain
**zutsū** headache

# Kana syllabet

rōmaji, hiragana, katakana

| a | あ (ア) | i | い (イ) | u | う (ウ) | e | え (エ) | o | お (オ) |
|---|---|---|---|---|---|---|---|---|---|
| ka | か (カ) | ki | き (キ) | ku | く (ク) | ke | け (ケ) | ko | こ (コ) |
| sa | さ (サ) | shi | し (シ) | su | す (ス) | se | せ (セ) | so | そ (ソ) |
| ta | た (タ) | chi | ち (チ) | tsu | つ (ツ) | te | て (テ) | to | と (ト) |
| na | な (ナ) | ni | に (ニ) | nu | ぬ (ヌ) | ne | ね (ネ) | no | の (ノ) |
| ha | は (ハ) | hi | ひ (ヒ) | fu | ふ (フ) | he | へ (ヘ) | ho | ほ (ホ) |
| ma | ま (マ) | mi | み (ミ) | mu | む (ム) | me | め (メ) | mo | も (モ) |
| ya | や (ヤ) | | | yu | ゆ (ユ) | | | yo | よ (ヨ) |
| ra | ら (ラ) | ri | り (リ) | ru | る (ル) | re | れ (レ) | ro | ろ (ロ) |
| wa | わ (ワ) | | | | | | | o | を (ヲ) |
| | ん (ン) | | | | | | | | |